"*Nobody's Mother* is a witty title for a brilliant work on first-century Artemis of the Ephesians. Sandra Glahn's encyclopedic research into the literary, epigraphic, and iconographic evidence brings the goddess into sharp focus, dispelling persistent myths. In accessible prose, Glahn persuasively argues that understanding Artemis is key to unlocking 1 Timothy 2:15's enigmatic phrase, 'saved through childbearing.' A must-read for students and scholars alike."

Lynn H. Cohick, distinguished professor of New Testament and director of Houston Theological Seminary at Houston Christian University, and associate editor of the *Dictionary of Paul and His Letters*, second edition

"*Nobody's Mother* is an impressive contribution to the discussion about women in church leadership and the background of 1 Timothy. With studious attention to archaeological and exegetical details, Sandra Glahn dives deep into some of the most complex questions surrounding one of the most complicated passages in the New Testament. Not every reader will agree with Glahn's conclusions, but everyone who is interested in what Paul was trying to say in 1 Tim 2:8-15 must wrestle with Glahn's scholarly, responsible work. I found this book very hard to put down!"

Preston Sprinkle, author, speaker, and host of the *Theology in the Raw* podcast

"In this masterful literary, epigraphic, architectural, and exegetical study, Sandra Glahn brings the significance of Artemis worship to bear in the interpretation of being 'saved through childbearing' (1 Tim 2:15). This text is critically linked to the seemingly transcultural prohibition of women teaching men (1 Tim 2:12). However, anyone seeking to be faithful to Scripture should remember that these texts were first God's Word to others before they were God's Word to us. By understanding who Artemis of the Ephesians was and how this likely influenced these texts, Glahn exposes the context of 1 Timothy to apply these words more accurately today. This book is a game changer."

Christa L. McKirland, theology lecturer at Carey Baptist College and executive director of Logia International

"It seemed highly unlikely to me that anyone could say anything fresh about 1 Timothy 2. Sandra Glahn has proven me wrong. With its close attention to material culture and biblical text, Glahn's evidence demands that we understand Artemis differently and therefore read this passage with fresh eyes. Immediately compelling through Glahn's honest personal narrative, *Nobody's Mother* kept me on the edge of my seat. I couldn't wait to see Glahn's conclusions. Now that I've read them, I know I'll be thinking about them, and changing how I teach this text, for a long time."

Amy Peeler, professor of New Testament at Wheaton College

"Paul's phrase 'saved through childbearing' becomes controversial to modern readers who approach the text from afar and yet attempt to apply it to their present contexts. An incorrect biblical interpretation leads to incorrect applications that, in some instances, like the one in this passage, bring devastating consequences for women who have had an unsupported and extrabiblical burden imposed on them. Sandra Glahn provides a unique cultural, historical, and theological understanding of this passage. In fact, *Nobody's Mother* is a masterful work that will remain the foundational text for understanding Artemis of the Ephesians and her implications in the biblical narrative. This work exemplifies how cultural, historical, and biblical scholarship serve the body of Christ worldwide."

Octavio Javier Esqueda, director of the PhD and EdD programs in educational studies and professor of Christian higher education at Talbot School of Theology, Biola University

"Sometimes biblical scholars don't know what they don't know. Then, like a restoration specialist removing layers of superfluous material to uncover the original beneath, a scholar unveils new research that cuts through old assumptions and suppositions. Sandra Glahn's meticulous exploration of Artemis of the Ephesians offers compelling and unavoidable scholarship necessary for every serious student of the New Testament. *Nobody's Mother* will revitalize the conversation around 1 Timothy and other Ephesus-related biblical writings."

Kelley Mathews, coauthor of *40 Questions About Women in Ministry*

"I appreciate this extensive study of Artemis from ancient sources that may not have been available to previous interpreters. Glahn's findings not only deconstruct some long-held views of the goddess, they also add depth to our knowledge of this leading deity in the social world of Ephesus in the first century. *Nobody's Mother* gives readers fresh perspective on texts like 1 Timothy 2:15 for modern interpretation by shining light on local, cultural realities that have previously lurked in the shadows."

Gary G. Hoag, author of *Wealth in Ancient Ephesus and the First Letter to Timothy*

"What a clear and compelling explanation for one of the most unclear passages in Scripture! This eye-opening book evaluates all the available evidence—literary, archaeological, and biblical—to help us better understand not only the historical context of Paul's words but also how the spiritual worth of a woman is not tied to the physical state of motherhood. Glahn's own story of infertility will encourage women in the modern church just as powerfully as her argument reframes women in first-century Ephesus."

Beth Allison Barr, James Vardaman Professor of History at Baylor University and author of *The Making of Biblical Womanhood: How the Subjugation of Women Became Gospel Truth*

NOBODY'S MOTHER

Artemis of the Ephesians
in Antiquity and the New Testament

SANDRA L. GLAHN

ivp
Academic
An Imprint of InterVarsity Press
Downers Grove, Illinois

InterVarsity Press
P.O. Box 1400 | Downers Grove, IL 60515-1426
ivpress.com | email@ivpress.com

InterVarsity Press® is the publishing division of InterVarsity Christian Fellowship/USA®. For more information, visit intervarsity.org.

Scripture quotations, unless otherwise noted, are from the NET Bible® copyright ©1996, 2019 by Biblical Studies Press, LLC. http://netbible.com. Used by permission. All rights reserved.

The publisher cannot verify the accuracy or functionality of website URLs used in this book beyond the date of publication.

Cover design: David Fassett
Interior design: Jeanna Wiggins

ISBN 978-1-5140-0592-7 (print) | ISBN 978-1-5140-0593-4 (digital)

Library of Congress Cataloging-in-Publication Data
A catalog record for this book is available from the Library of Congress.

29   28   27   26   25   24   23 | 13   12   11   10   9   8   7   6   5   4   3   2   1

To the giver of everlasting names

ISAIAH 56:4-5

CONTENTS

INTRODUCTION

AFTER MY AGING PARENTS SOLD their home and redistributed their belongings, I ended up with a hand-colored, monochromatic picture of one of my ancestors. I had seen the photo, but until I hung it on my wall, I had never known her name. At that time, I asked some family members about her.

One told me Julia was on my mother's side—probably through her mother. She came from Spain, having fled from there due to religious persecution. What persecution? When? How had she suffered? How did she end up in the Pacific Northwest? My mother and her mother and her mother before her were all courageous women. Was Julia the catalyst?

As much as I wanted to learn about my ancestor, the questions evoked a familiar sense of loss—the same one that has whispered grief to me for more than three decades. Although I'm the fourth of five kids and grew up expecting to have a large family of my own, I have a body that has treated at least eight embryos as a disease. I have never given birth.

I grew up in Oregon's Willamette Valley with two parents who loved me. While all families have their dysfunctions, I had what many would consider the ideal situation—a mom at home and a dad at the office.[1] My homemaking mother embraced what she saw as her calling. She

---

[1] I have told my story in multiple contexts. Readers can find a version of it as the foreword in Sue Edwards and Kelley Mathews, *40 Questions About Women in Ministry* (Grand Rapids, MI: Kregel Academic, 2022).

taught 4-H entomology (children in her club dubbed her "the Bug Lady"). She did YMCA mom-toddler swim lessons with us, following up with chocolate bars "for protein." And she helped us turn crayon shavings into stained-glass windows. I learned "Jesus Loves Me" sitting by her in church as she sang soprano with gusto. I watched as my mom taught herself watercolor painting. After looking at a mere sample, she could design and make a dress—sometimes even improve it. She was the kind of mom who made me the envy of fellow Camp Fire Girl campers, because while they were lucky to get mail, *I* got a whole care package.

I spent hours in Mom's and Dad's laps, listening to a book or hearing a song. From an early age I learned to can peaches, freeze asparagus, and sell pears that fell in our orchard. One night a week our family of seven would watch a TV show and eat popcorn. During the rest of our downtime, the five of us kids used our imaginations. We had a treehouse with real curtains, a log-cabin playhouse, a dog and a cat and some rabbits, a go-cart, and a one-acre garden. Because my mother was the only child of an only child, we even had my grandmother and her mother all to ourselves. Mom would bristle when people described her as a housewife. "I'm not married to the house," she would insist. "I'm a *home*maker."

Don't worry, I'll get to the academic part soon. This is relevant: the whole parenting gig looked great to me, seeing in my mother's vocation all I could ever want. So, by the time I married, I had embraced the roles of wife and mother as a woman's highest and best calling. Some of my perspective came out of appreciation for the home my parents had built. But some came from the broader culture, which had made *Fascinating Womanhood* a bestseller. The book laid out a vision for young women to marry and become like Amelia, Thackeray's "domestic goddess." After we moved to Arlington, Virginia, when I was ten, I heard about "ideal womanhood" at church. Think of Isabela from Disney's *Encanto* as a mom, and you get a sense of the impossible ideal.

My dad, who worked for the government, had applied for a transfer to Washington, DC, because he wanted to "expose his kids to culture"—at least that's how it was presented to me. Free Juilliard String Quartets and Smithsonian museums and National Geographic lectures lured my parents on an adventure they thought would last only a few years.

Down the street from our new house in a semiurban neighborhood was a Bible church with a great youth program. Our family attended a mainline denomination, but my parents let me attend worship wherever I wanted. So I joined that youth group. As I learned the Bible, I also absorbed all they taught and modeled about the nuclear family and how the father at the office and the mother at home was God's ideal distribution of labor.

After my sophomore and his junior year of college, I married Gary, my high-school sweetheart. I envisioned myself as a pastor's wife, with service to my husband, our children, and the congregation as my vocation. Just when I considered dropping out of college, though, Gary and his dad urged me to finish. Reluctantly, I stayed in school.

After Gary graduated, I again considered dropping out to put him through seminary. But he convinced me to finish while he taught high-school science, math, and biology. After I graduated, we moved to Texas, and I took a job to support him. He always had broader views about what I could do than I had for myself. I felt the need to assure friends and family that I had no aspirations to make a vocation of my work in human resources: I was employed with a financial services corporation only to "put hubby through."

Some expressed concern that my being the primary breadwinner would undermine Gary's manhood. I wondered about that too. But Gary insisted his manhood was not that fragile, and I noticed in the Scriptures that Jesus and the Twelve were supported by women's income (Lk 8:3).

Six years after we moved to Dallas, Gary graduated, so we decided it was time to expand our family. A year passed, and then another. I went to the doctor, who prescribed some pills. A third year. Nothing. And then it happened—a positive pregnancy test! I ran to the store to pick up steaks for what I envisioned as the best dinner of our lives. I borrowed a friend's china and set up the table by her pool so I could surprise my husband with the big news. He was going to have a new name: Dad.

But cheers turned to sobs when I miscarried.

"Seven pregnancy losses and an ectopic pregnancy requiring emergency surgery" sums up our second decade of marriage. My fluctuating hormones left me wondering who I really was. Meanwhile, my husband wondered what had happened to his happy wife, as he could barely reach me in my grief. During my final surgery—this one an emergency because of the ectopic pregnancy—I asked my doctor to tie my tubes. I saw my womb as a tomb for embryos and a danger to my health. Following my recovery, we moved forward with adoption.

We had three failed adoptions in three years.

Gary and I stood ready to lavish love on a child, yet every door to parenting slammed shut. Throughout that trauma, the most difficult part was not the losses themselves, excruciating as they were. The worst part was not even the financial, emotional, marital, or ethical crises that came with financing treatment, wondering if procedures would work, discovering how differently my husband and I processed grief, making love by the calendar, or navigating the ethics and cost of high-tech treatment. The hardest part was wondering what God had created me to do. Wasn't motherhood the ideal? If I could not procreate, what was my purpose?

I had come to believe, thanks to Aristotle by way of Aquinas, that a female is an undercooked male. I believed that a wife images God indirectly, through her husband—that her body was made for birthing, while a man's was made for thinking. Following that logic, my ideal of a woman said I would most fully image God by bearing and rearing children. But I now had no category for myself. Wasn't being a mother what God made wives for? In my own system, I failed to do the very thing for which I was created.

I had a mentor, Elizabeth, who gave me opportunities to teach the Bible. In doing so, I thrived. Beyond teaching women's Bible studies, I mentored wives of seminary students. I loved studying the Scriptures, teaching, and shepherding people. But in a way, thriving as a teacher only made matters worse. The Bible teachers I knew said women who wanted to teach had one outlet: "A woman will find her greatest satisfaction and meaning in marriage, not seeking the male role [i.e., Bible teaching], but in fulfilling God's design for her."[2]

I had read the commentators. Some said "saved through childbearing" (1 Tim 2:15 CSB) meant women were to channel their spiritual gift of teaching to raising of children. Up to that point I had assumed the scholars were right. But here I was, going through infertility, and I was processing my understanding of the passage considering all the single and infertile women with teaching gifts who were unable to fulfill such a mothering mandate.

Additionally, as a young Christian, I had heard a good sermon series on spiritual gifts. The speaker emphasized that such gifts were intended to benefit the entire body of Christ—not limited to one's relatives or friend groups. Some people had told me I possessed teaching gifts. I did love teaching the Bible, but if teaching my own children was supposed to be *the* outlet for my teaching, where did that leave me?

My husband and Elizabeth—both seminary graduates—urged me to study theology. A few years earlier, when the school they had attended opened its ThM degrees to women, I had objected. Why did women need

---

[2]Kelly Williams, "Biblical Conservatism and Women Pastors: A Southern Baptist Pastor's Understanding," *The Christian Post*, August 30, 2022, www.christianpost.com/voices/biblical-conservatism-and-women-pastors.html.

to learn the original biblical languages if not to use in the pulpit? I reasoned that seminary was for a man training to be a senior pastor—a vocation women were not designed to do. Nor did I have any desire to do so.

So, what was I made for? The spiritual wound from my apparent deficiency struck at the core of my womanhood. Wasn't a woman designed to mentor and teach the next generation through mothering? How could I live as an incomplete person?

Yet I saw that Paul encouraged some women to remain single (1 Cor 7:8). Were Mary and Martha deficient because they were presumably unmarried (Lk 10:38-42)? Why, if marriage and parenting is the end-all, be-all for a Christian woman, is Priscilla (also called Prisca) mentioned apart from any children she might have had (Acts 18:2-3, 19, 26; Rom 16:3-5; 1 Cor 16:19; 2 Tim 4:19)? The merchant of the Thyatira purple company, Lydia—did she even have a husband (Acts 16:14-15, 40)? Kids? Nympha, another house church leader (Col 4:15)—what about her? Where would she fit in an anthropology that equates biology with building the kingdom? And why in the world would Jesus have answered the woman who pronounced, "Blessed is the womb that bore you and the breasts at which you nursed!" with, "Blessed rather are those who hear the word of God and obey it!" (Lk 11:27-28). The virgins and widows who came after them—like Thecla, Felicitas, Agnes, Catherine of Alexandria, Catherine of Siena, Praxedes, and Pudentiana? What about them? Where did nuns come from if biological motherhood was God's ideal?

I thought I saw in the Bible that marriage is the ultimate outworking of God's male-female dynamic. And I saw the model of male as primary breadwinner and wife as stay-at-home mother rooted in sacred pages. Still, I noticed where Scripture contradicted my thinking. Even Proverbs 31, that passage seemingly describing ideal domesticity, didn't align. In it, the virtuous wife buys and sells merchandise (Prov 31:18), stretches forth her hand to the needy (Prov 31:20), sells belts in the marketplace (Prov 31:24), and—most shocking of all—teaches the *torah* of *hesed* (Prov 31:26). Aren't those the words for "Pentateuch" and "God's covenantal love"? Meanwhile, her husband is at the city gate (Prov 31:23). Does he even get paid? Where did my so-called ideal woman fit into such a system?

I had to know: What is a female human and what is God's vision for her? No less than a foundational biblical anthropology of woman was at stake. What was true, and what had the church picked up from the subculture and passed on to me? I needed to know how first-century authors would have answered this question and to see what they would have said about the idea of a woman created only for home and hearth. Secondary to the question about the primacy of marriage and stay-at-home motherhood was the appropriate outworking of the gift of teaching for a woman. I heard this:

> "Childbearing . . . represents the fulfillment of the woman's domestic role as mother in distinction from the man." Childbearing, then, is probably selected by synecdoche as representing the appropriate role for women. This rounds out the passage because a woman should not violate her role by teaching or exercising authority over a man; instead, she should take her proper role as a mother of children.[3]

Also, "When Paul says that a woman will be saved by childbearing, he means, therefore, that they will be saved by adhering to their ordained role."[4]

The referenced passage falls at the end of 1 Timothy 2. Its words were offered as the rationale for disallowing women's teaching or exercising the authority of men. Here's the passage, 1 Timothy 2:8–3:1, in an older and a newer translation, which have key differences:

> I will therefore that men pray every where, lifting up holy hands, without wrath and doubting. In like manner also, that women adorn themselves

---

[3]Andreas J. Köstenberger and Thomas R. Schreiner, eds., *Women in the Church: An Analysis and Application of 1 Timothy 2:9-15*, 2nd ed. (Grand Rapids, MI: Baker Academic, 2005), 259.
[4]Köstenberger and Schreiner, *Women in the Church*, 260.

in modest apparel, with shamefacedness and sobriety; not with broided [braided] hair, or gold, or pearls, or costly array; But (which becometh women professing godliness) with good works. Let the woman learn in silence with all subjection. But I suffer not a woman [or wife] to teach, nor to *usurp* authority over the man [or husband], but to be in silence. For Adam was first formed, then Eve. And Adam was not deceived, but the woman being deceived was in the transgression. Notwithstanding she [singular] shall be saved in childbearing, if they [plural] continue in faith and charity and holiness with sobriety. This is a true saying. (KJV, 1611; with author notes)

So I want the men in every place to pray, lifting up holy hands without anger or dispute. Likewise the women are to dress in suitable apparel, with modesty and self-control. Their adornment must not be with braided hair and gold or pearls or expensive clothing, but with good deeds, as is proper for women who profess reverence for God. A woman [or wife] must learn quietly with all submissiveness. But I do not allow a woman [or wife] to teach or *exercise* authority over a man [or husband]. She must remain quiet. For Adam was formed first and then Eve. And Adam was not deceived, but the woman, because she was fully deceived, fell into transgression. But she will be delivered through childbearing, if she continues in faith and love and holiness with self-control. This saying is trustworthy. (NET, 1996; with author notes)

Saved and *delivered through childbearing*. What do these words really mean? I had to know. If the primary outlet for a woman with the gift of teaching is parenting, having a baby should be a big priority. Does that mean a woman should try to have as many babies as possible? Such an idea might seem silly or at least strange. Yet the mother of a friend from Romania birthed sixteen children because her pastor taught that women had to continue bearing children to be saved, based on how he interpreted the verses above. I wondered, How have others understood the passage? Has the church through the centuries understood Paul to connect salvation with having big families?

All of this raised textual questions: Did the author of this influential document intend a universal application for every woman everywhere and always? Or did he intend a local application based on a timeless truth? Does his observation that the man was made first root a practice of female silence in the creation order, predating the fall? If so, does that make it a principle of creation order, rooted in the ideal state? And does it follow that men speaking with authority and women remaining silent is the for-all-time ideal? If so, how do we reconcile this principle of creation order with the Spirit filling women to prophesy in the church at Corinth (1 Cor 11:5)? Indeed, why did God call women to prophesy in every dispensation in which he called men to do so? Why was it a sign of the Spirit—instead of being a mark of male failure—on the day of Pentecost when both men *and* women, including girls, prophesied?

Praying (1 Cor 11:5). Prophesying (1 Cor 11:5). Being an apostle (Rom 16:7).[5] These actions and gifts all involve public speech. So why would God raise up women prophets like Miriam, Deborah, and Huldah, whose public proclamation included saying "thus saith the Lord" to men—even when good men were available? Add to these Junia, Elizabeth, Anna, Mary, and Phillip's daughters. What about the women in Corinth, whom Paul assumed would pray and prophesy in the assembly?[6] Why would Paul, only one chapter after saying what women should do with their heads when praying and prophesying, rank prophesying above teaching (1 Cor 12:28)—yet elsewhere prohibit all women from teaching (the lesser gift) while acknowledging that women will prophesy (the greater)? Didn't both involve public speaking in the church? Wasn't a "thus saith the Lord" of prophesy more like preaching than teaching?

---

[5] A full exploration of women in public ministry is beyond the scope of this book. For more on that subject, I recommend Sue Edwards and Kelley Mathews, *40 Questions About Women in Ministry* (Grand Rapids, MI: Kregel Academic, 2022).

[6] See Miriam (Ex 15:20), Deborah (Judg 4:4), Huldah (2 Kings 22:14), Junia (Rom 16:7), Elizabeth (Lk 1:41-45), Anna (Lk 2:36-38), Mary (Lk 1:46-55), Philip's daughters (Acts 21:9), and female prophets in Corinth (1 Cor 11:5).

It seemed that I needed answers to fundamental questions about what it meant and means to be saved through childbearing: Is the passage saying women should refrain from teaching truth in the presence of men because a woman's role of quietness is rooted in creation order as God's original ideal? Did "she will be saved through childbearing" (1 Tim 2:15 NRSV) relate to women in all churches throughout time? Or were the words to a specific recipient about his context, but with global ramifications—that is, handle false doctrine by silencing false teachers, but let them learn?

I needed to know. As I prayed about what to do, I did apply to seminary and was accepted. Yet I still worried: Was I pushing my way into a vocational world God intended only for men?

On the way out the door to my first class, I dropped to my knees in front of my couch, and I begged God to stop me if I was wrong. To my surprise these words from Jesus came to mind: "Mary has chosen what is better" (Lk 10:42 NIV). I thought of the story in which Jesus' quote appears, in a narrative I had barely thought about for months. Its context fit perfectly. Martha thought her sister was wrongly neglecting domesticity to learn theology, but Jesus had a different view of Mary's priorities.

I stood with confidence that day, and I walked out my front door and into the classroom. I had no idea where my seminary education would take me. I knew only that the first female seminarian was not feminist Betty Friedan's idea, but Jesus Christ's.

While at seminary, as I learned Greek and Hebrew, I saw many places where the human writers of Scripture had women in view, but I had missed their presence because translations had de-emphasized these women. For example, I had memorized, "The things that thou hast heard of me among many witnesses, the same commit thou to faithful **men**, who shall be able to teach others also" (2 Tim 2:2 KJV, emphasis mine). Seeing that the Greek said *anthrōpois*, or "people," I realized Paul had faithful *people* in view.

Then there was the passage that seemed to suggest I was undermining my husband's role of provider by putting him through seminary—the passage that says men who fail to provide for their families are worse than unbelievers (1 Tim 5:8). I was surprised to find the language was similarly inclusive. If someone (*tis*, τις) fails, *that person* is worse than an unbeliever. The word was broad enough to include both men and women. A few verses later, in the same context, the author even says a believing *woman* (*pistē*, πιστὴ) is to provide for her relatives (1 Tim 5:16). I double-checked with my Greek professor to make sure I was reading that correctly.

Observations such as these reinforced the big question: Was childbearing really the main spiritual outlet for a woman with the gift of teaching? What if that was a misinterpretation? If so, what did the author mean by "saved through childbearing"?

Answers to these questions would help answer the bigger questions about what God had made me—and other infertile women, single women, widows, and actually *all* women—to be and do. My anthropology of women was rooted in what I had thought was faithful exegesis. But the more I read in Hebrew and Greek, the more I saw how my anthropology of women had flaws.

Some people said to forget about the guy who wrote the words "saved through childbearing." He was confused, they said. But Paul was a brilliant scholar, theologian, and rhetorician. Two thousand years later, people across the world still marvel at his mind. It seemed unlikely that he would contradict himself within three chapters of a letter (1 Cor 11, 14).

Others wrote off Paul as a misogynist. But his greetings in Romans 16 are the opposite of those that would come from someone who devalues women. Phoebe was both a deacon of a specific church and his benefactor (Rom 16:1). Rufus's mother was a mom to him (Rom 16:13). Junia served jail time with him for the gospel (Rom 16:7). He mentions six more:

Prisca (Rom 16:3),[7] Mary (Rom 16:6), Tryphena and Tryphosa (Rom 16:12), Persis (Rom 16:12), Julia (Rom 16:15), and the sister of Nereus (Rom 16:15).[8]

Some said to disregard New Testament teaching about women's silence, because Paul couldn't help himself, living as he did in a culture steeped in patriarchy. Yet Paul also had vision of a different world (2 Cor 12:2). He had a highly developed eschatology. For him, the crucifixion and resurrection overturned the kingdoms of this world, and the change in male-female partnership served as a harbinger of things to come. To him, celibacy whispers of a world when procreation is unnecessary—no one dies. He himself chose to live without a loving partner to pursue his calling as the apostle to the Gentiles (Rom 11:13). Instead of setting up male-power structures, he chose words for influential people that are as devoid as possible of power: guardian (*episkopon*, ἐπίσκοπον; 1 Tim 3:2), servant/slave (deacon; 1 Tim 3:8, 12), and widow (1 Tim 5:9).[9]

I could not look at Scripture without addressing Paul. Others told me Paul was a product of his time and that he was simply trying to get the church to align with the culture—which rewarded women for having

---

[7]"Priscilla" is the Roman diminutive form of "Prisca," and the form that New Testament writers usually use when referring to Prisca (see Acts 18:2, 18, 26; 1 Cor 16:19; 2 Tim 4:19).

[8]Lucy Peppiatt observes that "many of Paul's fellow workers were women. . . . He was happy with women as leaders of house churches (Lydia in Acts 16 and Phoebe in Rom 16:1). We know of Priscilla and Aquila, who were both leaders and who both discipled Apollos in the faith (Acts 18:26), and Phoebe, who led a church at Cenchreae (Rom 16:1). Paul refers to his friend and coworker Junia as an apostle (Rom 16:7). Furthermore, he is clearly happy with women prophesying and praying in public in Corinth, and obviously approving of Phillip's four daughters, who were known as prophets (Acts 21:9). Given the way in which he describes the gift of prophecy as being that which edifies the *whole* church, and given that he elevates the gift of prophecy above the gift of teaching (1 Cor 12:28 is expressed in terms of priority and precedence: *first* apostles, *second* prophets, *third* teachers), it would seem strange for him to implement a contradictory practice that women should stay silent. This poses an immediate problem for the verses on silencing of women." Lucy Peppiatt, *Women and Worship at Corinth: Paul's Rhetorical Arguments in 1 Corinthians* (Eugene, OR: Cascade Books, 2015), 12.

[9]The church where Timothy ministers has so many widows (or man-less women—the term *widow* could refer to more than those bereft of husbands) that Paul advises him to divide their number into three groups. The neediest "actual" widows, were to go on "the list" and double as staff, providing they met qualifications. The requirement for widows on "the list" (or "enrolled," 1 Tim 5:9) to have been the wife of one husband parallels the requirement for a male overseer to be the "husband of one wife" (1 Tim 3:2). Paul did not advise marital or character requirements for general feeding of the hungry (Rom 12:20). See Sandra L. Glahn, "The 'Widow' in the Early Church: Marital Demarcation, Office Title, or Both?" Paper presented at the annual meeting of the Evangelical Theological Society, Fort Worth, Texas, November 18, 2021, www.wordmp3.com/details.aspx?id=40733.

children—for the sake of the church's witness. But Paul knew how to exegete something as basic as Genesis 1 and 2, and he could see past his own cultural context if he was going to be the apostle to the Gentiles.

I knew I needed to discern the difference between content written for an immediate audience—like avoiding meat sacrificed to idols (1 Cor 8)—and that which is applicable in every context for all time. I've never seen American Christians greet each other with holy kisses (2 Cor 13:12), and I can't take Paul's cloak to him in Troas (2 Tim 4:13). So how *do* we know when something is culturally bound?

I knew I needed scholars to help me understand—scholars who held a high view of Scripture, a fair view of Paul and his perception of gender, and whose explanations of 1 Timothy 2 accounted for all the interpretive factors which, to that point, looked like someone had tried to shoehorn them into fitting.

After earning my ThM, I went on to get my PhD with a focus on first-century backgrounds, especially as they relate to women. I also looked at history, tracing women and their contributions to the church for two thousand years. I found that the singular story I had been told about women (that is, "men have always held all the clergy roles") was incorrect. I found the widows and women deacons referenced in the church fathers and ecumenical council records—not to mention funerary inscriptions. I found the wives of male Reformers teaching, preaching, and burying the dead as expressions of the priesthood of all believers. I found Black women learning Greek and Hebrew alongside Black men in traditionally Black colleges—following in the tradition of Paula, Jerome's translation partner—long before White seminaries opened their doors to female students. Betty Friedan, a feminist impulse, or capitulating to culture had not started this after all. It was rooted in the design for gender parity, in imaging God himself.

* * *

Nobody's Mother is the book I wish I had had to help me address key questions about motherhood and teaching based on what it means to be saved through childbearing in 1 Timothy 2. But why the subtitle, *Artemis of the Ephesians in Antiquity and the New Testament*? What does Artemis have to do with it? In the quest to open doors for women in public ministry, some scholars in the past had said Paul's reference to childbirth was due to the influence of Artemis, an Ephesian goddess whom they associated with motherhood and fertility. But the view of Artemis as mother/fertility goddess had flaws. So, many scholars eliminated the "Artemis explanation" as an option. Yet in doing so, they lost other important background considerations relating to Artemis unrelated to her fertility or mothering—considerations that do help us better understand Timothy's world and Paul's concerns.

This book is for the reader who wants to avoid sacrificing a high view of Scripture while working to reconcile conflicting narratives about God's view of women. It's for the reader who sees Paul describe Priscilla as a fellow worker (Rom 16:3), notes that he says a wife has authority over her husband's body (1 Cor 7:4), and suspects the apostle has been misunderstood. It's for the person who looks at the history of the church and knows huge parts of the narrative—namely, the one about men and women partnering to do ministry—have gone missing. Or maybe they've seen that the Roman Catholic Church prohibits women from serving the Eucharist while having no major issue with women preaching. Meanwhile, Protestant rationale tends to be vice versa,[10] with women more likely to serve Communion than to preach. Why the difference?

This book is for the person who sees God giving spiritual gifts to women for the maturing of the body of Christ and has a hunch they're supposed to use them far beyond the nuclear family, important as that is.

---

[10]William G. Witt, *Icons of Christ: A Biblical and Systematic Theology for Women's Ordination* (Waco, TX: Baylor University Press, 2020), 19-40.

Even though I did not want to make women my go-to topic, I have heard from many who have found this research life-giving. So now I'm passionate about the subject, helping people—men and women alike—find answers to the same questions I had. Since the #MeToo and #ChurchToo movements, I've encountered even more people asking about women in public ministry, at the root of which is having a clear understanding of "saved through childbearing." Many confess that they have guarded the church doors against any form of feminism while leaving the back door wide open to misogyny.

I realize that I take a risk in sharing my journey at the beginning. The reader may say, "Your experience has led you to see the text a certain way." To which I would answer, "Of course. As has yours!" Everyone looks at the text through the grid of personal experience.

Nevertheless, it's true that we must always view our experience through the grid of the biblical text, not the other way around. Kathy Keller notes, "Unfortunately, I have often found that there is little theological reflection to follow the stories of personal journey."[11] Fair point. What follows my story, then, is chapters of theological reflection. My hope in sharing my own narrative is that it will put a human face on the questions we will explore in the pages to follow, expanding contemplation of the text to reach the realm of application that affects real people.

The issues considered in this work assume the inspiration of Scripture, but they question the validity of some *interpretations*.[12] The wideness in the range of interpretive options among those who love Scripture is exactly why my journey has taken me where it has.

So let's start at the very beginning. Woman was created in the image of God (Gen 1:27) and is ontologically equal to, rather than inferior to,

---

[11] Kathy Keller, *Jesus, Justice, and Gender Roles: A Case for Gender Roles in Ministry*, Fresh Perspectives on Women in Ministry (Grand Rapids, MI: Zondervan, 2012), loc. 637, Kindle.

[12] Some who believe the Scriptures urge women to public ministry are also among the strongest defenders of the authority of Scripture. A few who come to mind are F. F. Bruce, Gordon Fee, N. T. Wright, and Craig Keener.

man. In creation, woman was necessary as man's indispensable companion before God could pronounce the world to be "very good" (Gen 1:31). Whether she is single or married, divorced or widowed, with or without biological or adopted children, a woman has the same highest calling as every other human: to glorify God and multiply worshipers—that is, to do the will of God (Mt 28:19-20). This is what she was made for. This is a biblical anthropology. And this is the grid through which our interpretation will begin.

1

WHY TAKE
A FRESH LOOK?

As I've taught about women in public ministry for two decades, I have paid attention to the most common reasons people say they consider it unnecessary to take a fresh look at the biblical text on the topic. One might expect that in a seminary the reason would be Paul's statements about women (or wives) keeping silent in the churches (see 1 Cor 11; 14; 1 Tim 2). Yet the number-one reason I hear—maybe even *especially* among people with high levels of biblical literacy—is not textual. It's historical.

For many, the narrative has gone something like this: For two thousand years, the church has held a belief and observed a practice relating to women that has remained unchanged. But the influence of the Women's Movement in the United States has infiltrated the church, which has capitulated to culture. The idea that women can hold clergy positions and questions about women teaching biblical truth in public are *new*, influenced by one factor: feminism.

An author writing in *Recovering Biblical Manhood and Womanhood* (*RBMW*) put it this way when he described what he calls the historical understanding of Scripture: "This has been the view of historic orthodoxy to the present and, in fact, is still the majority view, though presently under vigorous attack. The very fact that its opponents call the view 'the traditional view' acknowledges its historic primacy. . . .

We should begin our discussion with the assumption that the church is probably right."[1]

The author does well to start with church history. The history of interpretation and practice relating to women is essential. That is why I, too, will start with it. But to be clear, the historical understanding relating to women was that "women were characterized as less intelligent, more sinful, more susceptible to temptation, emotionally unstable, incapable of exercising leadership."[2] William Witt notes a major shift from this position in recent decades: "Somewhere around the mid-twentieth century, the historic claims about women's essential inferiority and intellectual incapacity for leadership simply disappeared. Instead, all mainline churches—Catholic, Orthodox, Protestant, and Anglican—recognize the essential equality between men and women."[3] Some of the previous practices related to women have been rooted in an interpretation of Paul's statement that the woman, not the man, was deceived (1 Tim 2:14)—part of the very text we will explore.

A narrative about the history of ideas on the subject has filtered down from the academy to the masses. Consider the words of a blogger, who wrote this more than fifteen years ago: "It was the feminist teachings of the past few decades that first spurred Christians to try to argue for [women in public ministry]. Like it or not, the two schools of thought are intertwined."[4]

This is an incorrect origin story. But because such ideas so frequently shut down the topic, we will look first at the tradition. Here is a brief survey of some of the church's most influential voices.

---

[1]Lewis S. Johnson, "Role Distinctions in the Church: Galatians 3:28," in *Recovering Biblical Manhood and Womanhood: A Response to Evangelical Feminism*, ed. John Piper and Wayne Grudem (Wheaton, IL: Crossway, 2021), 212.

[2]William G. Witt, *Icons of Christ: A Biblical and Systematic Theology for Women's Ordination* (Waco, TX: Baylor University Press, 2020), 29.

[3]Witt, *Icons of Christ*, 29.

[4]Staci Eastin, October 8, 2010, www.writingandliving.blogspot.com. Blog no longer online.

INFLUENTIAL VOICES

John Chrysostom (347–407 CE), an early church father who served as archbishop of Constantinople, wrote, "The woman taught once, and ruined all. On this account therefore he [Paul] says, 'let her not teach.' But what is it to other women, that she suffered this? It certainly concerns them; for the sex is weak and fickle."[5]

Augustine of Hippo (354–430 CE) was a theologian, philosopher, bishop in North Africa, and one of fewer than forty people named as "doctor of the church." Many consider Augustine one of the most important figures of the Latin church in the Patristic Period. He wrote this: "[Satan made] his assault upon the weaker part of that human alliance, that he might gradually gain the whole, and not supposing the man would readily give ear to him or be deceived."[6]

We see similar ideas in the works of theologians in the Middle Ages. Bonaventure (ca. 1217–1274 CE), also named as a doctor of the church, was an Italian bishop, cardinal, scholastic theologian, and philosopher. He argued that only males could serve at the altar because women lacked the image of God, "but man by reason of his sex is 'imago Dei.'"[7]

Thomas Aquinas (ca. 1225–1274 CE) was a theological and educational doctor's doctor. His views on male and female were deeply influenced by those of Aristotle, who saw woman as "defective and misbegotten."[8]

Such ideas endured through the Renaissance. Desiderius Erasmus (ca. 1466–1536 CE) was a prominent Dutch philosopher and theologian. He said that that while woman was deceived by the serpent, man was

---

[5]John Chrysostom, "Homily 9 on 1 Timothy," in *Homilies on the Epistles to the Galatians, Ephesians, Philippians, Colossians, Thessalonians, Timothy, Titus, and Philemon*, ed. and trans. Philip Schaff, *NPNF* 1/13.

[6]Augustine, *The City of God and Christian Doctrine*, trans. Philip Schaff, *NPNF* 1/2.

[7]Bonaventure, *Commentarium in IV Libros Sententiarum Magistri Petri Lombardi*, Opera Omnia, answer C, https://womenpriests.org/theology/bonav1-bonaventure/.

[8]Thomas Aquinas, *Summa Theologiae*, trans. Fathers of the English Dominican Province, 2nd ed. (1920), First Part, Question 92, Reply to Objection 1, https://www.newadvent.org/summa/1092.htm.

impervious to such beguilement: "The man could not have been taken in either way by the serpent's promises or by the allure of this fruit."[9]

Of the Protestant reformers, who celebrated the priesthood of all believers, the most influential was German priest, theologian, and author Martin Luther (1483–1546 CE). Rather than seeing male mastery of the woman as rooted in the fall, Luther believed that "by divine and human right, Adam is the master of the woman. . . . There was a greater wisdom in Adam than in the woman."[10]

The next generation of Reformers taught similarly. Here's an example: John Knox (ca. 1514–1572 CE), founder of the Presbyterian Church of Scotland, was a theologian and writer who described women as "weak, frail, impatient, feeble and foolish" as well as "inconstant, variable, cruel and lacking the spirit of counsel and regiment."[11]

This is no random sampling of obscure theologians. Some tremendously influential leaders whom the church has revered through the centuries (and still does) held unbiblical views of women. William Witt, in *Icons of Christ*, observed: "Historically, there is a single argument that was used in the church against the ordaining of women: women could not be ordained to the ministry (whether understood as Catholic priesthood or Protestant pastorate) because of an inherent *ontological* defect. . . . Moreover, this argument was used to exclude women not only from clerical ministry, but from all positions of leadership over men, and largely to confine women to the domestic sphere."[12]

The ontological-defect argument of traditionalists is why a segment of Christian believers in the United States began to call themselves

---

[9]Erasmus, *Collected Works of Erasmus: Paraphrases on the Epistles to Timothy, Titus and Philemon, the Epistles of Peter and Jude, the Epistle of James, the Epistles of John, and the Epistle to the Hebrews*, trans. John J. Bateman, ed. R. D. Sider (Toronto: University of Toronto Press, 1994), 44:17.

[10]Martin Luther, "Lectures on 1 Timothy," in *Luther's Works*, ed. Hilton C. Oswald (St. Louis: Concordia, 1973), 28:278-79.

[11]John Knox, "Section Two: The First Blast to Awake Women Degenerate," in *The First Blast of the Trumpet Against the Monstrous Regiment of Women* (1558; repr., London: 1878), www.gutenberg.org/files/9660/9660-h/9660-h.htm.

[12]Witt, *Icons of Christ*, 21.

complementarians rather than *traditionalists.* Unlike the men quoted above, complementarians affirm that, on an ontological level, woman is equal with man. Complementarians make the following affirmation in the Danvers Statement: "Both Adam and Eve were created in God's image, equal before God as persons and distinct in their manhood and womanhood (Gen 1:26-27; 2:18)."[13] Such a pronouncement was a break with tradition. Yet on the foundation of traditionalist views of woman's ontology, practices for society, church, and home were built.

WHAT WOMEN ACTUALLY DID

If the practice of women serving in public leadership did not originate with feminists such as Betty Friedan, Gloria Steinem, and Bella Abzug, when did such practices start? They began before the American and French Revolutions, with their calls for freedom and individual rights. One call for women to lead was a pamphlet by Margaret Fell (later married to Quakerism founder George Fox) written in 1666. Titles were longer in her day. Here is hers: "Womens Speaking Justified, Proved and Allowed of by the SCRIPTURES, All such as speak by the Spirit and Power of the Lord JESUS. And how WOMEN were the first that preached the Tidings of the Resurrection of *JESUS*, and were sent by CHRIST'S Own Command, before he ascended to the Father, *John* 20. 17."[14] Lithographs of women preaching often accompanied such writings, depicting events that predated the Women's Movement by two hundred and fifty years. Yet the evidence points still earlier.

The Protestant reformers in the sixteenth century emphasized the priesthood of all believers. That movement included women such as

---

[13]From the Council for Biblical Manhood and Womanhood (CBMW) website: "The Danvers Statement summarizes the need for the Council on Biblical Manhood and Womanhood (CBMW) and serves as an overview of our core beliefs. This statement was prepared by several evangelical leaders at a CBMW meeting in Danvers, Massachusetts, in December of 1987. It was first published in final form by the CBMW in Wheaton, Illinois in November of 1988." "The Danvers Statement," CBMW .org, https://cbmw.org/about/danvers-statement/

[14]Fell's punctuation has been retained.

Katharina Schütz Zell, who preached at her husband's funeral and wrote in defense of women in ministry.[15] But one might notice, even earlier, *The Book of the City of Ladies*, written by the widow Christine de Pizan. She was born in the 1300s. Each time one explores an earlier period, the sources point back to prior sources. Here's a sampling from earlier centuries, with the most recent first.

- Pope Paschal I (Rome; West; ca. 822 CE)—For the Basilica of Santa Prassede, Rome, Pope Paschal I had a mosaic made of his mother, Theodora, which included a label in stone describing her as "*Theodo[—] Episcopa*." Elsewhere in the church, an inscription refers to her as "Lady Theodora Episcopa." Some tesserae in the mosaic have been replaced, removing her name's feminine ending to make it say "Theodo[—] Episcopa." But the matching inscription confirms the mosaic's original wording: "Theodora Episcopa." The word *episcopa* is often translated "bishop" or "elder." If the pope identified his mother as *episcopa*, why would someone later change the evidence?

- The Council of Trullo (Constantinople; East; 692 CE)—In canon 14, the council speaks of ordination (*cheirotonia*) for women deacons using the same term used for ordination of priests and male deacons.

Two local synods in Gaul speak of the diaconate of women for their region:

- Fourth Ecumenical Council (Chalcedon; East; 451 CE)—in canon 15, an earlier minimal age of sixty years for women deacons was relaxed to forty years. The earlier practice was based on 1 Timothy 5:9: "Let a widow be enrolled if she is not less than sixty years of age" (ESV).

---

[15]For a short summary of the lives and theology of Protestant reformers Katharina Schütz Zell and Marie Dentière, see Catherine T. Arnsperger, *Two Reformation Women and Their Views of Salvation: Katharina Schütz Zell and Marie Dentière* (Mesquite, TX: Aspire Productions, 2020).

- First Council of Nicaea (Nicaea; East; 325 CE)—in canon 19, deacon[esse]s[16] are mentioned in passing in a canon referring to the reconciliation of ex-members of the sect of Paul of Samosata (ca. 260–272 CE). Paul, Patriarch of Antioch, denied the three Persons of the Trinity: "In this way one must also deal with the deacon[esses] or with anyone in an ecclesiastical office."

The evidence goes back further still.[17] In *TDNT* the last entry under the meaning of *widow* references an office with the title *widow* in the early church.[18] In *The Ministry of Women*, Gryson asserts, "One thing is undeniable: there were in the early Church women who occupied an official position, who were invested with a ministry, and who, at least at certain times and places, appeared as part of the clergy. These women were called 'deaconesses' and at times 'widows.'"[19]

---

[16]In the same way English lacks differentiation between teacher and teachess or plumber and plumbess with masculine and feminine endings, the Greek language at the time of the earliest Christians had no distinct feminine form of *diakonos*. The Greek noun *diakonos* can apply to women. For this reason, I am putting in brackets the suffix *-ess* in *deaconess*—so "deacon[ess]."

[17]A sampling of secondary sources on church history as it relates to women: Roger Gryson, *The Ministry of Women in the Early Church* (Collegeville, MN: Liturgical Press, 1976); Bonnie Bowman Thurston, *The Widows: A Women's Ministry in the Early Church* (Minneapolis: Fortress, 1989); William Weinrich, "Women in the History of the Church: Learned and Holy but Not Senior Pastors," in *Recovering Biblical Manhood and Womanhood: A Response to Evangelical Feminism*, ed. John Piper and Wayne Grudem (Wheaton, IL: Crossway Books, 1991), 329-51; Susanna Elm, *Virgins of God: The Making of Asceticism in Late Antiquity* (Oxford: Clarendon Press, 1994); Ute E. Eisen, *Women Officeholders in Early Christianity: Epigraphical and Literary Studies*, trans. Linda M. Maloney (Collegeville, MN: Liturgical Press, 2000); Kevin Madigan and Carolyn Osiek, eds. and trans., *Ordained Women in the Early Church: A Documentary History* (Baltimore, MD: Johns Hopkins University Press, 2011); Lynn H. Cohick, *Women in the World of the Earliest Christians: Illuminating Ancient Ways of Life* (Grand Rapids, MI: Baker Academic, 2009); Lynn H. Cohick and Amy Brown Hughes, *Christian Women in the Patristic World: Their Influence, Authority, and Legacy in the Second through Fifth Centuries* (Grand Rapids, MI: Baker Academic, 2017); Witt, *Icons of Christ*; Leanne M. Dzubinski and Anneke H. Stasson, *Women in the Mission of the Church: Their Opportunities and Obstacles Throughout Christian History* (Grand Rapids, MI: Baker Academic, 2021); Joy A. Schroeder and Marion Ann Taylor, *Voices Long Silenced: Women Biblical Interpreters Through the Centuries* (Louisville, KY: Westminster John Knox, 2022).

[18]See Augustine, *The City of God and Christian Doctrine*, trans. Philip Schaff, *NPNF* 1/2. An older version of *TDNT's* entry for Χήρα, or "widow," lists "Widows as an Institution in the Community" and ends with this note: "Because of their work in the church they are highly honored, have a special place at worship on the left behind the presbyters (as deacons are on the right behind the bishop), receive communion after the deacons and before subdeacons, etc. Yet by the end of the early period the order disappears. It perhaps finds a new form in the monastic orders for women, for nuns take up many of the duties that widows originally discharge." Gustav Stählin, "Χήρα," in Walter Bauer, William F. Arndt, and F. Wilbur Gingrich, "*chēra* [widow]" in *A Greek-English Lexicon of the New Testament and Other Early Christian Literature* (Chicago: University of Chicago Press, 1957), 462.

[19]Gryson, *The Ministry of Women*, xi.

One must never think the US Women's Movement single-handedly introduced the idea that women belonged in the public, vocational, ordained ministry of the church. To say such an impulse started in the United States or that it started with feminism misrepresents history. It was *not* the feminist teachings of the past few decades that first spurred Christians to argue for women in public ministry. In fact, the impulse began in the church on the day of Pentecost, when a sign of the Spirit—not a sign of male failure—was the public proclamation of men and women together proclaiming that God was doing a new thing.

So, if women once held church office, what happened?

WHAT LED TO THE DECLINE?

Four key reasons for the decline of women in public ministry emerge from researching the topic:

1. **Redefining priesthood:** A shift away from emphasizing the priesthood of all believers (1 Pet 2:9) led to an all-male priesthood in the pattern of the Old Testament. The church looked to the past rather than the future kingdom in its view of the telos of men and women.[20]

2. **Shift toward infant baptism:** The major shift away from adult baptism toward infant baptism eliminated the need for women's "assistance at the baptism of women for reason of decency."[21]

3. **Law/Temple:** The church tended to return to ceremonial aspects of the law with accompanying temple practices—especially after Constantine. With physical church buildings came an increasing clergy-laity divide that treated worship structures as temples. With a shift from the believer's body to a physical structure as the

---

[20]See Cynthia Long Westfall, *Paul and Gender: Reclaiming the Apostle's Vision for Men and Women in Christ* (Grand Rapids, MI: Baker Academic, 2016), 143-76. Westfall is one of the few authors who has addressed the topic of women in church leadership in light of eschatology and Scripture's kingdom vision for men and women.

[21]Gryson, *The Ministry of Women*, 113.

temple of God came a return to some physical-temple regulations that affected females, such as barring menstruating women from worship. Madigan and Osiek, in *Ordained Women in the Early Church*, write, "The motif of blood as uncleanliness unworthy of the purity of the altar . . . was one of the most common reasons given for the exclusion of women from altar service, once the celebration of the Eucharist acquired the connections with cultic purity that accompanied the understanding that it replaced Temple sacrifice."[22]

4. **Anthropology:** Greek views of women's nature influenced Christian leaders, who concluded that women were weak, fickle, lightheaded, of mediocre intelligence, and a "chosen instrument of the devil." The considerations "which supported the traditional argument in the ancient writers often reflect an anthropology which could not be unanimously admitted today."[23]

Each of these four factors can be challenged with Scripture.

The historical record includes unbiblical practices rooted in misinformation about women. The record also demonstrates precedent for women holding public office in the church. Thus, fresh looks at the textual and background information are in order.

SOCIAL-HISTORICAL REASONS
TO TAKE A FRESH LOOK

In addition to textual and historical reasons to revisit the question about women in public leadership, eight factors also point to the need for a fresh look.

Revelations from archaeology. Developments in archaeology have provided scholars with excellent background information that can help readers understand the contexts in which texts were written and

---

[22]Madigan and Osiek, *Ordained Women in the Early Church*, 139
[23]Gryson, *The Ministry of Women*, 112.

received.[24] For example, the story of Justa,[25] preserved for posterity when Mount Vesuvius erupted in 79 CE, contains clues about slavery, women, adoption, manumission, and Roman law. Fragments found in Herculaneum contained a dossier of a legal challenge involving Justa that took place four years before the eruption. Her case provides social clues about the abovementioned topics, all of which New Testament writers mention. It would appear, for example, that adoption in the Greco-Roman world had a stronger association with inheritance than adoption has in the West today.

In nearby Pompeii, erotic art helps social scientists better understand prostitution and its practices. Classics professor Marguerite Johnson describes murals from brothels and buildings that served as brothels—inns, lunch counters, and taverns—that show fair-skinned prostitutes with stylized hair.[26] Johnson's observation that prostitutes' hair was stylized, drawn from the visual evidence, reveals that prostitutes' hair was not shaved. This information helps interpreters understand the apostle Paul's statement, "For if a woman will not cover her head, she should cut off her hair. But if it is disgraceful for a woman to have her hair cut off or her head shaved, she should cover her head" (1 Cor 11:6). Commentators have suggested the apostle was pointing to a cultural practice of prostitutes shaving their heads.[27] But

[24]For example, see Paul Weaver, "Archaeological Discoveries of Ancient Corinth and the Exegesis of First Corinthians: From Archaeology to Exegesis," *The Journal of Ministry & Theology* 23, no. 2 (Fall 2019): 204-5. Also, E. Metzger, "The Case of Petronia Iusta," *Revue Internationale des Droit de l'Antiquité (3rd series)* 47 (2000): 151-65.

[25]Jane F. Gardner, "Proofs of Status in the Roman World," *Bulletin of the Institute of Classical Studies,* no. 33 (1986): 1-14.

[26]Marguerite Johnson, "The Grim Reality of the Brothels of Pompeii," *The Conversation,* December 12, 2017, https://theconversation.com/the-grim-reality-of-the-brothels-of-pompeii-88853. See also Sarah Levin-Richardson, *The Brothel of Pompeii: Sex, Class, and Gender at the Margins of Roman Society* (Cambridge: Cambridge University Press, 2019).

[27]For example, James Burton Coffman, *Commentary on 1 Corinthians 11,* Coffman's Commentaries on the Bible (Abilene, TX: Abilene Christian University Press, 1983–1999); Lucy Peppiatt, *Women and Worship at Corinth: Paul's Rhetorical Arguments in 1 Corinthians* (Eugene, OR: Cascade Books, 2015), 99; Dio Chrysostom, Discourse 64, section 2: "Just so, Cyprus too had its Demonassa, a woman gifted in both statesmanship and law-giving. She gave the people of Cyprus the following three laws: a woman guilty of adultery shall have her hair cut off and be a harlot—her daughter became an

archaeological evidence suggests no such connection. Shaved heads were more likely associated with publicly shaming an adulteress.

More specific to Artemis's influence, archaeology at the Ephesus ruins in Turkey is relevant to how one understands 1 Timothy 2 since the recipient was in Ephesus. Immendörfer notes, "Up to the end of the nineteenth century, only literary texts were available as sources on ancient Ephesus. Today, they are still consulted as the basis for historical studies," but "archaeological excavations have given an entirely new dimension to the research of ancient Ephesus."[28]

More time for study. Many of our ancestors worked in agrarian settings six or seven days a week in contexts in which clothes washing and fruit picking happened by hand. These hard-working souls enjoyed no bank holidays. But with the advent of electric dishwashers (1920s), dryers (1937), clothes washers (1908), and even harvesting machines (1892), many—especially women—have time to focus less on surviving and more on learning. Technology has allowed for more choices in how humans spend time,[29] which some use to pursue knowledge. More women pursuing learning has led to changes in perceptions of what women can do. More women looking at the biblical text with knowledge of original languages has led to new insights.

Longer life expectancy. Along with having more time, people are living longer. Even if mothers stay home with children, they can raise their kids, launch them, and have decades-long careers. One of my colleagues taught until he was ninety-five years old. Consider that a woman with a similar constitution starting as late as age forty-five might still have

---

adulteress, had her hair cut off according to the law, and practiced harlotry" (*Orations*, trans. Henry Lamar Crosby, Loeb Classical Library [Cambridge, MA: Harvard University Press, 1940]). In the case of the woman described by Dio Chrysostom, it appears that she had her hair cut off due to adultery, followed by living the life of a harlot. Such a practice differs from a harlot having the practice of shaving her head.

[28]Michael Immendörfer, *Ephesians and Artemis: The Cult of the Great Goddess of Ephesus as the Epistle's Context*, Wissenschaftliche Untersuchungen zum Neuen Testament II 436 (Tübingen, Germany: Mohr Siebeck, 2017), 78.

[29]Marcelo Gleiser, "Does Technology Make You Freer?," *Cosmos & Culture* (blog), NPR.org, October 21, 2015, www.npr.org/sections/13.7/2015/10/21/450473648/does-technology-make-you-freer.

a fifty-year career. If she worked while raising a family or if she never had a husband or children—true of a growing number of women—she might have six or seven decades on which to build knowledge.[30] Longevity is allowing for more human processing of information, more mentoring, and the cultivated passing on of knowledge.

The internet. The World Wide Web has brought growth in the number and availability of sources. With the influx of women in history departments, the focus of topics has expanded.[31] One historian writes, "In drawing our attention to the world beyond high politics, women's historians were part of a broader group of 'social historians' who argued that the social and cultural practices we take for granted in fact have a history, and one which we need to understand."[32] New academic fields with more collaborations and easier updates have added to accessible sources of knowledge. The addition of Google Translate in 2006 made many additional sources accessible for researchers, allowing for distance collaboration.

Several decades ago, a scholar in Boston might write a letter in English and mail it to a translator to render into French. This scholar with a translation could send it by snail mail to Paris and wait six weeks for a reply. Once received, the information in French could be mailed for translation into English, which could then be read and processed. A reply would go through the same cycle. Writing for *Computers and Society*, Joseph Fulda said, "Perhaps the most obvious benefit to scholarship wrought by the Internet is its facilitation of scholarly efforts. . . . Being more convenient, it is more likely to be engaged in altogether and

---

[30]"In 1900, one in forty Americans died annually. By 2013, that rate was roughly one in 140, a cumulative improvement of more than two thirds. . . . Life expectancy at birth rose by more than 30 years over this period, from 47 to 79." "Mortality in the United States: Past, Present, and Future," *Penn Wharton Budget Model*, June 27, 2016, https://budgetmodel.wharton.upenn.edu/issues/2016/1/25/mortality-in-the-united-states-past-present-and-future.

[31]Judith Zinsser, *History and Feminism: A Glass Half Full* (New York: Twayne, 1993).

[32]Nicole Bourbonnais, "A Brief History of Women's History," *Engenderings* (blog), London School of Economics, March 29, 2016, https://blogs.lse.ac.uk/gender/2016/03/29/a-brief-history-of-womens-history/.

if the time available to the project is decreased only partially because of the facilitation, it is possible that the remaining time will be used to enhance the quality of the effort."[33]

Today, scholars using the internet can locate an obscure piece of research published in another language, run it through Google Translate, read it, craft a clarifying question for its author, get that message translated online, research the scholar's contact information on his or her university's website, and email a message before going to sleep. Upon rising, they might find a reply in their inbox, which can be instantly translated and read over cereal and coffee.

Access to more research coupled with the ability to collaborate with scholars across the world has exponentially increased the amount of data available and the ability to build on others' work. Whereas earlier scholars had to camp out in libraries, one can now sit at home in comfortable clothes and search archives for Anatolian digests and works by specialists in Roman attire. While scholars of the past had to leave when the library closed, today's researcher has access to sources around the clock.

Consequently, biblical scholars have more information about the contexts in which the earliest believers received sacred texts. And because of videoconferencing platforms, experts can interact in real time, vetting each other's work before it reaches the public.

Access to education leading to more emphasis on social history. Past recountings of history tended to feature women who were members of the upper class and politically connected, such as Cleopatra; Helena, empress of the Roman Empire; and Catherine the Great. Historians tended to focus more on empire, political history, and conquest.

The influx of women doing academic work in history has influenced the questions and expanded the subject matter in areas that directly aid studies of historical backgrounds in both Testaments. An

---

[33]Joseph S. Fulda, "The Internet as an Engine of Scholarship," *Computers and Society* 30, no. 1 (March 2000): 17.

effect is the demand for more accessible primary documents. One scholar wrote, "The past twenty years have seen enormous advances in making important primary records accessible . . . resulting in numerous specialized bibliographies; increased numbers of primary source reprint series; increasingly organized and indexed archival sources making topics pertaining to women more easily accessible."[34] An example of this is the work of Lynn Cohick and Amy Brown Hughes in *Christian Women in the Patristic World*.

Social historians are asking different questions. These might include: What did head coverings mean? Did prostitutes shave their heads? Did people shave the head of an adulterer? What were the male/female authority structures? Were gods and goddesses perceived as competing, or did they specialize in death or nature or love? More and better data now exist to help answer questions about the average life expectancy, diet, apparel, and how long it took to travel from Ephesus to Rome.

Past scholars knew little about middle- and lower-class life. Even more than in ancient Rome and Smyrna—which today are covered by modern streets, shops, and homes in Rome and İzmir—places preserved in stone, ash, or mud are providing enormous amounts of evidence. The ruins at places such as Ephesus, Pompeii, and Herculaneum are providing troves of knowledge about the everyday lives of middle- and lower-class people in the first century.

Because the most translated, distributed, and accessible collection of first-century documents from everyday people—a veritable gold mine of social-history info—is the New Testament, biblical scholars now have more diversity in the academic disciplines shedding light on the text. New Testament scholars are interacting with art historians and social historians and vice versa, and this has led to more informed conclusions.

---

[34]Gerda Lerner, "Priorities and Challenges in Women's History Research," *Perspectives on History*, American Historical Association, April 1, 1988, www.historians.org/research-and-publications/perspectives -on-history/april-1988/priorities-and-challenges-in-womens-history-research.

Pointing up at a depiction of a woman at Jesus' feet, a guide I once overheard walking a group through the UNESCO mosaics in Ravenna's Basilica of Sant'Apollinare Nuovo said, "For years we thought she was the woman caught in adultery. Now we think she's the woman with the issue of blood. See how she reaches for Jesus' robe?" Art historians with high levels of visual literacy collaborate with textual scholars with high levels of biblical literacy, and together they draw on shared strengths to assess more accurately what they see.

While we know that in first-century Judea and Samaria patriarchal thinking was the norm, we also now know that limitations were more fluid for Greek women and even more so for women in Rome. A female in Ephesus had yet more freedom, and an Egyptian woman, the most autonomy of all. Thus, often people living in the same era in different locales had differing norms.

Developments in epigraphy and papyrology. The wording of many inscriptions is now available for searches in online concordances, unavailable before the internet. Such technologies make it possible for scholars to search by word, phrase, and geographic location without having to pore over books in distant libraries or read them at the actual sites.

More than half a million Greek, Latin, and Semitic inscriptions have survived from the Hellenistic and Roman periods[35]—the exact period of interest to biblical scholars—with most inscriptions having yet to be incorporated into our lexicons. And more inscriptions are being discovered every year. Staggering potential exists for updates to dictionaries of Koine Greek and Latin.

Ten years ago, a scholar had to do all his or her own inscription translations. Now someone can read English translations of inscriptions found in Ephesus about women in the first century.

---

[35]D. Clint Burnett, *Studying the New Testament through Inscriptions: An Introduction* (Peabody, MA: Hendrickson Academic, 2020), 165.

Developments in literary analysis. With better access to primary sources, one can do better literary analysis. For example, in the past, when an ancient writer complained that women were too talkative, scholars have tended to take such statements at face value. Today's historian, however, has the benefit of more contextual clues. When reading a writer such as Cicero, who used woman imagery to insult Antony in *The Second Philippic*, a contemporary scholar might consider how Cicero used gender as part of his rhetorical strategy. The historian might ask such questions as, "Is Cicero making an observation about what is generally true in his world, or is he including his negative assessment as part of a stereotype to insult Antony's enemies?"[36]

Perhaps of more relevance to a New Testament scholar, historians are asking, "Did Strabo have an agenda when he mentioned that Corinth used to have temple prostitutes?" In answer to this question, Stephanie Budin wrote *The Myth of Sacred Prostitution in Antiquity.* She and other scholars countered the views of those asserting that cult[37] worship in Greek and Roman temples involved fertility goddesses and temple prostitution.[38] Budin's work has taken another look at Near Eastern, Greco-Roman, and early Christian texts. She argues that most of the sources once thought to pertain to sacred prostitution have no connection to the practice and have been grossly misunderstood.[39] Today's scholar is more apt to consider the number of years separating an ancient writer from the event that he (it was usually a "he") describes. In the first century, Strabo described cult prostitution in Corinth's distant past (from his perspective)—another factor that has led

---

[36]Nancy Myers, "Cicero's (S)Trumpet: Roman Women and the Second Philippic," *Rhetoric Review* 22, no. 4 (2003): 337-52.

[37]Throughout this work I use the word *cult* not as something "extremist or false, with its followers often living in an unconventional manner under the guidance of an authoritarian, charismatic leader," but as "a system or community of religious worship and ritual." (See "cult," *The American Heritage Dictionary of the English Language,* https://ahdictionary.com/word/search.html?q=cult.)

[38]Antonio Varone, *Eroticism in Pompeii* (Los Angeles: J. Paul Getty Museum, 2001), 90; Everett Ferguson, *Backgrounds of Early Christianity,* 2nd ed. (Grand Rapids, MI: Eerdmans, 1993), 64.

[39]Stephanie Budin, *The Myth of Sacred Prostitution in Antiquity* (New York: Cambridge University Press, 2008), 209.

archaeologists to consider as hearsay such statements in the absence of evidence to support them.

Better data about semiotics. Another development is the explosion of findings in the field of semiotics, which looks at symbols and signs as elements of communicative behavior. A ring worn on the fourth finger may communicate something different in the United States than in Europe. What one thinks of a man wearing a baseball cap at a funeral falls in the field of semiotics. In the West, a long, white dress on a woman's wedding day says something different from what a red mini-skirt might express. In terms of studying the ancient world, developments in semiotics include knowing how and where a woman covered her head, with what she covered it (a veil, hair, and/or fillets), and what doing so expressed in her context. When the apostle Paul told the Corinthians he had put away childish things (1 Cor 13:11), he might have been including actual apparel that marked him as a minor.

Further, deeper readings of ancient texts have led to seeing women hidden between the lines. Since Octavian passed laws allowing exemption from *manus* (male supervision) for citizen mothers of three children, the historian today may observe that "exemption as incentive" suggests women preferred freedom to being under authority. Also, the very existence of such a law indicates some women lived free of male authority.

CONCLUSION

I'm not saying Scripture changes based on culture, nor am I saying Scripture contradicts itself. In fact, because it does not do so, I believe scholars might be able to reconcile some passages that appear to contradict each other. They can do so by considering differing audiences and contexts in which words were written and read—because every biblical text has a literary, historical-cultural, and social context. Knowing this helps readers to understand its meaning.

Sometimes meaning is difficult to discern—so one uses clear passages to interpret difficult passages. And how scholars handle narrative passages differs from how they read a statement of principle. For example, David used five smooth stones to kill Goliath, but that does not mean the prophet who recorded the story meant for readers to find in those stones "David's five principles of leadership."

I'm also not saying Paul needs updating. *Paul* is not who needs an update—*we* do, considering that the tools used for interpretation have *already been updated*. They can help us find where many interpretations of the same texts have varied among those who hold a high view of Scripture. Such updated tools can also help in places where scholars have guessed about semiotics, such as the meaning of a woman's shaved head.

The past half century alone has seen enormous developments—from the wealth of literary information to archaeological, epigraphic, and iconographic evidence. Our understanding of backgrounds has exploded, affecting how we interpret texts, including texts about women. And all these factors point to the need to revisit the data.

It is time we used these gifts given to our generation to help us more accurately handle the Word of truth. Because, as my Greek professor, Daniel B. Wallace, taught us: "If Jesus is the truth, we should never be afraid to explore where the truth might lead."

2

THE STORY OF EPHESUS
IN STONE AND SCRIPTURE

PAUL WAS WRITING TO TIMOTHY IN EPHESUS (1 Tim 1:2-3), and the apostle had some instructions relating to women and men, or perhaps wives and husbands. So, what was Timothy's context, and what did Paul know of it when he wrote the words about women's silence and childbearing? What was going on in Ephesus, where Timothy was located?

A BRIEF HISTORY OF THE CITY

Ephesus was a port city with access to great roads and harbors. When Augustus became emperor (27 BCE), he replaced Pergamum with Ephesus as the capital of proconsular "Asia"—what today is Western Asia Minor. Ephesus's new status made it both the seat of the governor and a major center of commerce. It was strategic geographically, politically, and—of special relevance to this topic—religiously.

The city was the guardian of Artemis's temple, a major banking center and one of the Seven Wonders of the Ancient World. It was also guardian of the Roman imperial cult. And it became an important site of early Christianity. One can see this in the New Testament itself: Priscilla and Aquila, Paul's partners in tent making and ministry, moved to Ephesus with him (Acts 18:19); for two years and three months, the city served as a base for Paul (Acts 19:8, 10; ca. 50–53 CE). And en route to or from Ephesus, Paul probably wrote

1 Corinthians (see 1 Cor 16:8), Ephesians, and 1 and 2 Timothy. The addressee of the latter two, Timothy, continued to minister in Ephesus even after his mentor had departed (1 Tim 1:3). And one of the seven churches of Revelation is Ephesus (Rev 2:1-7).

That's what Scripture itself says. But tradition adds more. It places Jesus' mother in Ephesus along with the elder John after his exile on Patmos in the '90s.[1] Thus, the Gospel of John is thought to have been written in Ephesus, and the elder John is believed to have written 1, 2, and 3 John to nearby communities of believers. That's a lot of influence by Ephesus on the New Testament.

EPHESUS: THE DISTURBANCE

Acts 19 gives readers the most extended, specific narrative establishing the city's religious context at the time of the earliest Christians. Sorcerers burned magic books (Acts 19:18-20), Paul taught daily in a lecture hall (Acts 19:9-10), and an uprising made the apostle decide to end his time in the city earlier than planned (Acts 19:23–20:1). The problem? Serious opposition from followers of Artemis.

In the verses below from Acts 19:19-22, notice how deeply embedded Artemis's cult is, both in the city and across the empire. Note, too, how an uprising of the goddess's followers causes Paul to expedite his departure plan (emphasis mine):

> Large numbers of those who had practiced magic collected their books and burned them up in the presence of everyone. When the value of the books was added up, it was found to total 50,000 silver coins. In this way the word of the Lord continued to grow in power and to prevail.
>
> Now after all these things had taken place, Paul resolved to go to Jerusalem, passing through Macedonia and Achaia. He said, "After I

---

[1] Both Irenaeus (*Against Heresies* 3.1.1) and Eusebius of Caesarea (*Church History* 3.1) say that the apostle John came to Ephesus, where he worked and died. The assumption is made that since Jesus charged John with his mother's care from the cross (Jn 19:25-27), John took Mary with him to Ephesus. An ancient Church of St. Mary does exist in Ephesus and dates to the early 400s, which coincides with the Third Ecumenical Council (431), which declared Mary to be *Theotokos*—Mother of God.

have been there, I must also see Rome." So *after sending two of his assistants, Timothy and Erastus, to Macedonia,* he himself stayed on for a while in the province of Asia.

After this, as Luke[2] records it, a silversmith who profited from selling silver shrines of Artemis gathered workers in similar trades and reminded them that Paul had persuaded people across their province that "gods made by hands are not gods at all" (Acts 19:26). This worker saw Paul's ministry as a threat both to profits and to Artemis's temple, not to mention the renown of the goddess herself.

Upon hearing this, the workers grew enraged and shouted, "Great is Artemis of the Ephesians!" (Acts 19:28). Fervor spread across the city, and a crowd rushed into the 25,000-seat theater. Two of Paul's Macedonian traveling companions, Gaius and Aristarchus, got dragged in, but the disciples and some provincial authorities who liked Paul kept out the apostle. Most of the confused members of the crowd didn't even know why they had gathered (Acts 19:32); some thought it was about Alexander, because some Jews had pushed him to the front. But when Alexander gestured that he wanted to speak, *"they recognized that he was a Jew,"* and "they all shouted in unison, *'Great is Artemis of the Ephesians!'* for about two hours" (Acts 19:33-34; emphasis added).

The city clerk quieted the crowd, asking them a rhetorical question: "Who does not know that [Ephesus] is the keeper of the temple of *the great Artemis* and of her image that fell from heaven?" (Acts 19:35; emphasis added). This clerk urged people to lodge any complaints through proper channels, lest they be charged with rioting (Acts 19:40), a serious offense, and sent them home. Meanwhile, Paul gathered the disciples, bid them farewell, and departed for Macedonia.

One can see here that Ephesus lies in the grip of magic and Artemis worship, Paul has sent Timothy on ahead to Macedonia, and Jewish

---

[2]Traditionally, authorship of Luke–Acts is attributed to Luke.

people are already on the Ephesians' bad side (Acts 19:33-34). At this point in nascent Christianity people still consider followers of Jesus to be a sect within Judaism.

Paul must have later sent Timothy back to Ephesus, because within the first lines of his first epistle to Timothy, Paul writes, "As I urged you when I was leaving for Macedonia, stay on in Ephesus to instruct certain people not to spread false teachings" (1 Tim 1:3). One might wonder what sort of false doctrines Paul had on his mind when writing to Timothy with strategies for ongoing pastoral care.

ARTEMIS OF EPHESUS

Acts 19 provides clues as to the false doctrines: the goddess Artemis here bears the moniker "of the Ephesians" added to her name. She is worshiped both in Ephesus and throughout Asia. Her temple and cult are linked to the city's economy. Her temple has great renown. Her followers prioritize her honor. And they know that something relating to the goddess is Zeus-fallen (*diopetous*, διοπετοῦς; Acts 19:35).[3]

Thus, the New Testament itself reveals a major religious context from which false teaching of concern to Paul likely originated: the Artemis cult. This background information did not originate with archaeology or inscriptions or linguistics or secular feminism. Scholars working in these disciplines do confirm details that appear in the book of Acts. But the idea that the religious setting in Ephesus might inform Paul's instructions to Timothy in his epistles to his protégé comes straight out of the Acts of the Apostles. Scripture helps interpret itself.

For hints about what challenges Artemis's followers might have brought to the church, one needs to know what followers of Artemis

---

[3]*Dios* is the Greek word for Zeus/Jupiter.

believed. What was Timothy up against? Were local teachings about origins and creation, deception, women and men, and childbearing on Paul's mind when he crafted warnings?

A husband-and-wife team, the late Drs. Catherine and Richard Kroeger, wrote a book, *I Suffer Not a Woman: Rethinking 1 Timothy 2:11-15 in Light of Ancient Evidence*, to answer some of these questions.[4] They borrowed their title, "I Suffer Not a Woman," from the KJV text of 1 Timothy 2:12. The Kroegers asserted that the main goddess in Ephesus, Artemis of the Ephesians, was a mothering fertility goddess. Such being the case, they concluded that Paul's instruction about women teaching was written to counteract the teachings of Artemis's ancient fertility cult, which they said included temple prostitution. The Kroegers saw Paul's statement about the woman being deceived, coupled with his statement about prohibiting women's speech, as the apostle's solution for dealing with a local problem. They concluded that the apostle's phrase about being saved through childbirth was part of his apologetic against an ancient fertility cult involving sacred prostitution.[5]

Looking at the literature, one can see how scholars building on the Kroegers' work might have come to believe Artemis in first-century Ephesus was a fertility goddess—to which they attributed Paul's focus on childbearing.[6] One scholar who holds this view described the Ephesian Artemis, saying, "As the mother goddess, Artemis was the source of life, the one who nourished all creatures and the power of fertility in nature."[7]

---

[4]Richard Clark Kroeger and Catherine Clark Kroeger, *I Suffer Not a Woman: Rethinking 1 Timothy 2:11-15 in Light of Ancient Evidence* (Grand Rapids, MI: Baker, 1992).

[5]Kroeger and Kroeger, *I Suffer Not a Woman*, 70, 98.

[6]Scholars on both sides of the complementarian/egalitarian divide have said this. See, for example, Robert L. Saucy and Judith K. TenElshof, eds., *Women and Men in Ministry: A Complementary Perspective* (Chicago: Moody Publishers, 2001), 284; Scot McKnight, *The Blue Parakeet: Rethinking How You Read the Bible*, 2nd ed. (Grand Rapids, MI: Zondervan, 2018), 199.

[7]Linda L. Belleville, "Teaching and Usurping Authority," in *Discovering Biblical Equality*, 2nd ed., ed. Ronald W. Pierce and Rebecca Merrill Groothuis (Downers Grove, IL: InterVarsity Press, 2004), 220.

Figure 2.1. The "Beautiful Artemis" (125–175 CE), Ephesus Archaeological Museum, Selçuk, Turkey. Photo by Sue Edwards.

The argument goes something like this: Artemis as depicted in Ephesus had many breasts (see fig. 2.1). Breasts relate to mothering and fertility. So Artemis must be a mother goddess. Because the Amazons are deeply connected with the city's history, the combination of the mother-fertility goddess and Amazon man-hating gave the city an over-emphasis on the female principle. In the Kroegers' assessment, a proto-Gnostic view prevailed among converts from the Artemis cult, and Paul was trying to put a stop to their practice of male-female role reversal.

This argument received bad reviews. Reputable Ephesus scholars discredited their conclusions,[8] with key concerns being doubt about the Amazon connection, the lack of evidence connecting Artemis with mothering or fertility, and the late dates for the sources used. Oster observed that *polymaston*, or "many-breasted"—a word used to describe Artemis of the Ephesians—appeared only in late, polemical Christian sources.[9] Jerome, writing in the fourth century CE, was one of these.[10] Another respected Ephesus scholar asserted that a connection between

---

[8]For example, Robert A. Pyne, "I Suffer Not a Woman: Rethinking 1 Timothy 2:11-15 in Light of Ancient Evidence," *Bibliotheca Sacra* 150, no. 598 (April–June 1993): 247-48. See also "Three Reviews of *I Suffer Not a Woman* by Richard and Catherine Kroeger," in Wayne Grudem, *Evangelical Feminism and Biblical Truth* (Sisters, OR: Multnomah, 2004), 646-74.

[9]Richard Oster, "Ephesus as a Religious Center under the Principate, I. Paganism before Constantine," in *Aufstieg und Niedergang der Römischen Welt*, ed. Wolfgang Haase and Hildegard Temporini, (New York: Walter de Gruyter, 1990), 1725.

[10]Tertullian quotes Minucius Felix's *The Octavius* (early third century CE) as saying, "Diana sometimes is a huntress, with her robe girded up high; and as the Ephesian she has many and fruitful breasts." *Ante-Nicene Fathers*, "Fathers of the Third Century: Tertullian," Part Fourth; Chapter XXI, The Octavius of Minucius Felix, trans. Philip Schaff (1819–1893), www.tertullian.org/fathers2/ANF-04/anf04-34.htm accessed February 27, 2023.

Ephesus and the Amazons, whom he considered mythical, lacked support.[11] The bad reviews sent a message: in the first century, no such pro-woman mentality in Ephesus existed.

Other scholars, rather than pointing to late dates in connecting Artemis with mothering, pointed to early ones. They saw Artemis as a conflation with a mother goddess in Anatolia dating between the fifth and seventh centuries BCE.[12] But this assertion had the same problems with dates: the evidence was too far removed from the time of the earliest Christians to assure scholars that such thinking was still present at the time of Paul and Timothy. It appeared that some had created a "synoptic construct" when describing Artemis, whose identities across time had been conflated.[13] What Bible interpreters really needed to know was: Who was Artemis of the Ephesians *in the world of Paul and Timothy?*

Many scholars have downplayed any Amazon connections, but open-air stone carvings in a temple in Ephesus dedicated to the emperor Hadrian tell a different story. The reliefs date to about 138 CE—within 100 years of Paul and Timothy—and they feature Amazon women as integral to the city's origins.

Although sources seeing Artemis as many-breasted had late dates, and the idea of her as an Anatolian mother goddess had a very early date, one can establish that the Amazon connection was present at the time of the earliest Christians. The reliefs tell how these warrior women came from south of the Black Sea and founded Ephesus, which they named for their leader.

---

[11]Lewis S. Johnson, "Role Distinctions in the Church: Galatians 3:28," in *Recovering Biblical Manhood and Womanhood: A Response to Evangelical Feminism*, ed. John Piper and Wayne Grudem (Wheaton, IL: Crossway, 2021), 212.

[12]For example, Theodora Jenny-Kappers, *Muttergöttin und Gottesmutter in Ephesos: von Artemis zu Maria* [*Mother Goddess and Mother of God in Ephesos: from Artemis to Mary*] (Einsiedeln, Switzerland: Daimon, 1986).

[13]Oster is source for the "synoptic" description. See Oster, "Religious Center," 1661-1728. "Conflate" was LiDonnici's assessment of Oster's summary; Lynn R. LiDonnici, "The Images of Artemis Ephesia and Greco-Roman Worship: A Reconsideration," *Harvard Theological Review* 85, no. 4 (Oct 1992): 390.

Many have described the Amazons as mythological. But archaeologists in the mid-1990s unearthed evidence of actual warrior women who lived near the Black Sea. The late American archaeologist Jeannine Davis-Kimball found their remains on the plains of Kazakhstan. TammyJo Eckhart, writing about Davis-Kimball's find, observed, "She discovered kurgans, burial mounds, in which both male and female skeletons were found buried with weapons, arrow heads and daggers. . . . The graves could be identified as belonging either [sic] Scythian, Sauromatian, or Sarmartian nomads living in the region between the seventh and fourth centuries BCE."[14]

Later, *Smithsonian Magazine* reported on the excavation, saying:

> The trail of the Amazons nearly went cold after Herodotus. Until, that is, the early 1990s when a joint U.S.-Russian team of archaeologists . . . found over 150 graves belonging to the Sauromatians and their descendants. . . . There were graves of warrior women who had been buried with their weapons. One young female, bowlegged from constant riding, lay with an iron dagger on her left side and a quiver containing 40 bronze-tipped arrows on her right. The skeleton of another female still had a bent arrowhead embedded in the cavity. . . . On average, the weapon-bearing females measured 5 feet 6 inches, making them preternaturally tall for their time. . . . To the Greeks, the Scythian women must have seemed like incredible aberrations, ghastly even. . . . Strong, resourceful, and brave, these warrior women offer another reason for girls "to want to be girls" without the need of a mythical Wonder Woman.[15]

About the same time, *National Geographic* ran an article in which an expert on the Amazons said, "The Greeks were both fascinated and appalled by such independent women" and depicted them "as beautiful, active, spirited, courageous, and brave." The article goes on to note that

---

[14]TammyJo Eckhart, "An Author-Centered Approach to Understanding Amazons in the Ancient World" (PhD diss., Indiana University, 2007), 187.

[15]Amanda Foreman, "The Amazon Women: Is There Any Truth Behind the Myth?," *Smithsonian Magazine*, April 2014, www.smithsonianmag.com/history/amazon-women-there-any-truth-behind -myth-180950188/.

"Quite a few of the losers in duels are shown gesturing for mercy. But among Amazons, not so much. We have about 1,300 or so images of Amazons fighting. And only about two or three of them are gesturing for mercy. So they're shown to be extremely courageous and heroic."[16]

Ample evidence exists from the late empire period that Ephesus indeed had a strong connection with the Amazon women. In the literary record, Strabo (63 BCE–23 CE), a Greek geographer, philosopher, and historian, cites both the Amazon version and the alternate story of Ephesus's founding. Possibly, both narratives circulated simultaneously, or people held to one or the other in the same era. In the iconographic record, statues of Amazon women stood for centuries in the temple of Artemis in Ephesus—one of which, rediscovered in the late nineteenth century, would have been there at the time of the earliest Christians.[17]

In considering what cultural factors might have influenced Paul's instructions to Timothy, one must consider that the influence of Amazons might have been among them—especially because in addition to the stone reliefs in Ephesus, Strabo and others associated these women with the Artemis cult there. And one question leads to many more: If the Amazon narrative affected beliefs, how did they do so? Even if the Amazons were not connected with temple prostitution or mothering or fertility, who were they? Did Paul have concerns about women that related to false teaching coming from worshipers of the goddess Artemis with an Amazon connection? If Artemis *and* her Amazonian devotees were single, did the women in Ephesus seek to emulate their city's founders and the goddess they worshiped by remaining unmarried? If so, might that explain Paul's advice that young Ephesian widows should marry (1 Tim 5:14)—counsel that stands in

---

[16]Simon Worrall, "Amazon Warriors Did Indeed Fight and Die Like Men," *National Geographic*, October 28, 2014, www.nationalgeographic.com/history/article/141029-amazons-scythians-hunger-games-herodotus-ice-princess-tattoo-cannabis.

[17]See Karl L. H. Lehmann-Hartleben, "The Amazon Group," *Parnassus* 8, no. 4 (April 1936): 9-11.

contrast with his advice to Corinthian widows, who he thought should remain single (1 Cor 7:8)? Might a strong virginity mindset explain why the church in Ephesus, influenced by Gentile converts, was so full of single females that Paul needed to divide widows into three groups—younger women and two groups of older women, divided according to financial need (1 Tim 5:3-16)?

To understand who Artemis was in Paul and Timothy's day, one must examine the origin stories to which authors contemporary to Paul kept referring. These questions come at an opportune time, as several decades have passed since the Kroegers wrote *I Suffer Not a Woman*. Since then, archaeologists have uncovered many new inscriptions and artifacts, and heated debate has calmed down enough for scholars to approach the data with more openness. Epigraphic evidence uncovered in Ionia and across the ancient world has also become more accessible.

A deep dive into the primary sources is required—beginning with papyri, moving to inscriptions, and ending with statues and visual images. What do the primary sources say about Artemis's background? Who was she at the time of the earliest Christians? And how might knowing the answer shed light on what it means to be "saved through childbearing"?

3

ARTEMIS IN THE LITERARY SOURCES

KNOWING THE MYTHOLOGY about Artemis is essential to understanding her cult and its interaction with the earliest Christians in Ephesus. Greek mythology for Gentiles in the apostle's world provided a backdrop of polytheistic belief much like monotheism provides a backdrop of belief for Christians.

What follows is a survey of what the best-known primary sources, such as Homer and Pliny, said about the goddess. Special attention is given to mentions of her in connection with Ephesus. The sources are listed in chronological order by author with a few pertinent journals and reference books also included, including those on classical Greek mythology.

It's helpful to know that Zeus is Artemis's father, his wife is Hera, and his lover is Artemis's mother, Leto. Artemis and her twin, Apollo, are the children of Zeus and Leto. Their dalliance explains why Hera is less than fond of their children.

WRITERS IN ANTIQUITY

Attributed to Homer, ca. eighth century BCE[1]

Iliad 5.70: This story hints of Artemis's ability as a forest-dweller, archer, and healer: "Skamandrios . . . a mighty huntsman and keen lover

---

[1]Quotations from *The Iliad* are from Homer, *The Iliad*, trans. A. T. Murray, 2 vols. (Cambridge, MA: Harvard University Press, 1924), available through www.perseus.tufts.edu.

of the chase. Artemis herself had taught him how to kill every kind of wild creature that is bred in mountain forests, but neither she nor his famed skill in archery could now save him."

Iliad 5.445-50: Brief mention is made of Artemis having the ability to heal: "There Leto and the archer Artemis healed him [Aeneas] in the great sanctuary and glorified him."

Iliad 6.205: Bellerophon's daughter is described as "slain in wrath by Artemis of the gold reins."

Iliad 6.425-26: Andromache tells of how her family died, including this detail: "And my mother, that was queen beneath wooded Placus . . . in her father's halls Artemis the archer slew her." Apparently, Artemis killed Andromache's mother after Achilles released her for ransom. Here Artemis is a wrathful killer.

Iliad 9.530-42: In an oft-quoted story,[2] Homer describes Artemis, daughter of Dios (Zeus), as golden-throned and vengeful after being slighted by a mortal king. He offered first fruits to all of the gods except Artemis. Angry when offended, Artemis has power to cause soldiers to fight one another: "For golden-throned Artemis had driven this evil on them, angry that Oineus [king of Kalydon] had failed to give the pride of the orchards, first fruits, to her. To the rest of the gods he had offered due sacrifice; but alone to this daughter of great Zeus, he had given nothing. He had forgotten—or had not thought, in his great delusion. So in wrath at his whole mighty line, the lady of arrows sent on them the fierce wild boar with shining teeth, who after the way of his kind did much evil to the orchards of Oineus."

Iliad 16.183: Artemis is described as "huntress of the golden arrows and the echoing chase."

---

[2]See also Statius, *Thebaid* 2.469 (Roman epic, first century CE); Seneca, *Troades*, 827 (Roman tragedy, first century CE); Diodorus Siculus, *Library of History* 4.34.2 (Greek historian, first century BCE); Pseudo-Hyginus, *Fabulae* 172, 174 (author, first century BCE to first century CE); Pseudo-Hyginus, *Astronomica* 2.7; Ovid, *Metamorphoses* 8.269 (Roman epic, first century BCE to first century CE); Pseudo-Apollodorus, Bibliotheca 1.66 (Greek mythographer, second century CE); Antoninus Liberalis, *Metamorphoses* 2 (Greek mythographer, second century CE); Pausanias, *Description of Greece* 7.18.8 (Greek travelogue, second century CE).

Iliad 19.59: Achilles wishes that Artemis had killed the girl Briseis instead of letting this girl become a point of contention between himself and Agamemnon. Artemis is depicted as one who would kill a girl.

Iliad 20.40: The gods who fought on the side of Troy are listed: Apollo, "Artemis the Archer," Aphrodite, Leto, and Xanthus. Artemis is a warrior, adept with bow and arrow.

Iliad 20.39, 71: When the gods enter the battle for Troy, "against Hera, the huntress of the golden arrows [Artemis] stood forth, and the echoing chase, even the archer Artemis, sister of the god that smites afar." (No love lost here between Hera and Artemis.)

Iliad 21.470-95:[3] Artemis, described as "queen of the wild beasts, Artemis of the wild wood," fights Hera, who takes the opportunity to chide "the archer queen," asking how she dares as a "bold and shameless thing." Hera says, "It was against women that Zeus made you a lion and granted you to slay whoever of them you wished," and advises that it is better for Artemis to slay beasts than fight someone mightier than her. Hera then "took the bow and its gear from [Artemis's] shoulders. And with these same weapons, smiling the while, [Hera] beat [Artemis] about the ears."

Zeus made Artemis "a lion" with the ability to kill whoever she wants, which Hera sees as an action against women. Notice Homer's description of Artemis as queen of the wild beasts, associated specifically with deer; as queen of the wood; and as archer queen, who carries a quiver with arrows.

It is worth noting here that the apostle Paul told the Corinthians, "I fought with wild beasts[4] at Ephesus" (1 Cor 15:32). Commentators have wondered if he meant people or literal animals. Interestingly, Paul used a form of the same word for beasts[5] that Homer uses here to describe

---

[3]Homer, *Iliad* 21.470-95.
[4]The word used is: ἐθηριομάχησα; bold added for ease of comparison with Homer's word choice.
[5]Homer's word choice: πότνια θηρῶν.

Artemis as the master of wild beasts. Elsewhere in the New Testament, the author of Acts describes how Paul faced great difficulty because of Artemis's followers (Acts 19:23-41). Perhaps we find in Homer's description of Artemis an explanation for Paul's meaning when he describes fighting beasts.

Iliad 21.505-11: "When she [Leto] had taken her daughter's bow and arrows, went back; but the maiden [Artemis] came to Olympus, to the house of Zeus" and wept on her father's knee. Zeus, laughing gently, asked which god had mistreated her. "The fair-crowned huntress of the echoing chase" told him Hera was to blame. Artemis is described as "fair crowned."

Iliad 24.600-609: The goddess Niobê, in her hubris, bragged that she had twelve children—six sons and six daughters—but Leto, the mother of Artemis and Apollo, bore only twins. To punish Niobê for her arrogance, Apollo killed all her sons with a silver bow while "arrow-pouring" Artemis killed all her daughters. Note how this aligns with the statement attributed to Hera that Artemis is especially keen to kill females.

The number of Niobid children varies according to the storyteller. Homer says they are twelve; Euripides and Apollodorus say fourteen; Herodotus, four; Sappho, eighteen. Others say twenty. Regardless of the number, half are always sons and half daughters. Using arrows to put Niobê in her place, Apollo and Artemis team up to render the arrogant Niobê childless. This is hardly nurturing or mothering behavior: "The daughters, the arrow-pouring Artemis [killed], because Niobê had considered herself equal to fair-cheeked Leto, claiming Leto had borne only two children while she herself was mother to many. And so those mere two destroyed them all."

Far back in Artemis's history, she is perceived as a powerful, volatile sovereign who determines who will live or die. She has no affinity for children or women.

Hymn 9 to Artemis 9.1-5:[6] Artemis, brought up with Apollo, is said to be a far-shooter who delights in arrows. She has an all-gold horse-driven chariot.

Hymn 3 to Apollo 3.5-19:[7] Leto's children are described as "lordly Apollo and Artemis shooter of arrows—her in Ortygia, him brought forth in Delos the rocky" while their mother in labor "reclined on a great tall peak of the Kynthian highland, close to a date-palm tree." Artemis is said to have been born in Ortygia, which is near Ephesus, while Apollo was born in Delos. The twins' differing places of birth are about 400 miles apart.

Hymn 3 to Apollo 3.94-130:[8] Leto in labor is "racked nine days and nine nights with pangs beyond wont." And with her are "all the chiefest of the goddesses" except Hera. "Only Eilithyia, goddess of sore travail [midwifery], had not heard of Leto's trouble," because Hera had bewitched her.[9] When the midwife, Eilithyia, finally "set foot on Delos, the pains of birth seized Leto, and she longed to bring forth."

As Artemis was born first, she is presumed present at the birth of Apollo, her twin. The *Theogony* ("Birth of the Gods"), by the poet Hesiod (eighth to seventh century BCE), elsewhere describes how some gods were born with full use of their faculties. Perhaps the best-known example is Athena, who emerges from Zeus's head full grown, wearing armor.[10] Watching her mother labor for nine days is possibly what motivates Artemis to ask Zeus to make her a perpetual virgin (see Callimachus, below).

---

[6]Homer, "Hymn 27 to Artemis," in *The Homeric Hymns and Homerica*, trans. Hugh G. Evelyn-White (Cambridge, MA: Harvard University Press, 1914), 9.1-5.

[7]Homer, "Hymn 3 to Apollo," in *The Homeric Hymns and Homerica*, trans. Hugh G. Evelyn-White (Cambridge, MA: Harvard University Press, 1914), 3.5-19.

[8]Homer, "Hymn 3 to Apollo," 94-130.

[9]Apollo is cleaned, wrapped, and fastened with a gold band. Leto does not suckle him; instead, he is nourished on nectar and ambrosia.

[10]Hesiod. *Theogony*, 901 in *The Homeric Hymns and Homerica*, trans. Hugh G. Evelyn-White (Cambridge, MA: Harvard University Press; London, William Heinemann Ltd. 1914). www.perseus .tufts.edu/hopper/text?doc=Perseus%3Atext%3A1999.01.0130%3Acard%3D901, accessed February 27, 2023.

Hymn 27 to Artemis 27.1-22:[11] Homer describes Artemis as a "modest virgin, the deer-shooter profuse of arrows . . . sister to Apollo of the golden sword." In "mountains and windy heights" she "takes her pleasure in the hunt and draws her golden bow to discharge grievous arrows." She has an "intrepid heart" which "turns every way, killing the animals' brood." Other descriptions of her call her an "animal-watcher, profuse of arrows," who carries a "bent bow and goes to the great house of Apollo to "organize the Muses' and Graces' fair dance." There, Artemis "hangs up her bent-back bow and her arrows . . . her body beautifully adorned, leading the dances."

Artemis is described as a modest virgin and beautifully adorned. One wonders if the emphasis on the Ephesian goddess's modesty and beautiful adornment were on Paul's mind when he wrote his exhortation that women be modestly adorned (1 Tim 2:9).

Odyssey 5.120-24:[12] Calypso reminds Hermes how chaste Artemis kills Orion with her painless arrows. Notice that causing a painless death is attributed to Artemis.

Odyssey 6.109: After a feast, Artemis and her maidens "threw off their head-gear and fell to playing at ball." While they sang, Artemis was "joying in the pursuit of boars and swift deer" while Leto looked on with pleasure. Artemis was said to be easily identified, because "though all are fair—so amid her handmaidens shone the maid unwed."

Artemis and all her maidens wear headgear (perhaps a headband across their foreheads—which might have marked them as virgins).

Odyssey 6.150-51: Nausikaa is a character in Homer's *Odyssey* who is said to be second only to Artemis in beauty and stature. This detail reveals how Artemis was perceived.

Odyssey 11.172: Odysseus encounters the ghost of his mother in the Underworld and asks if she died of illness or by the euthanizing

---

[11]Homer, *Homeric Hymns*, 27.1-22.

[12]References from *The Odyssey* come from Homer, *The Odyssey with an English Translation*, trans. A. T. Murray, Loeb Classical Library (Cambridge, MA: Harvard University Press, 1919).

arrows of Artemis: "Come, tell me this, and declare it truly. How did you die? Was it long disease, or did the archer, Artemis, assail you with her painless shafts and slay you?" This is the second reference to Artemis euthanizing.

Odyssey 11.324-25: Artemis killed Ariadne on the island of Dia: "Artemis slew her in sea-girt Dia because of the witness of Dionysus." Once again, we see Artemis killing a woman.

Odyssey 15.409-12: Artemis accompanies her brother to the island of Syria, where he kills the aged painlessly with euthanizing arrows.

Odyssey 15.476-79: Artemis kills another woman. As the story goes, when a pig farmer was a child, Phoenicians kidnapped him with the help of his wicked nurse. "Then Artemis, the archer, smote the woman, and she fell with a thud into the hold, as a sea bird plunges."

Odyssey 17.37; 19.54: Homer describes wise Penelope as being lovely as Artemis or golden Aphrodite.

Odyssey 18.185: Penelope, mourning her husband, Odysseus, wishes Artemis would euthanize her: "Would that chaste Artemis would even now give so soft a death that I might no more waste my life away with sorrow at heart, longing for the manifold excellence of my dear husband. . . . Artemis, mighty goddess, daughter of Zeus, would that now you would fix your arrow in my breast and take away my life. . . . Would that those who have dwellings on Olympus would blot me from sight, or that fair-tressed Artemis would smite me, so that with Odysseus before my mind I might even pass beneath the hateful earth."

Herodotus, ca. 484–ca. 425 BCE

The History 1.26:[13] King Croesus received his kingdom at age thirty-five. He is said to have "attacked the Ephesians first. The Ephesians then, being besieged by him, dedicated their city to Artemis and tied a rope from the temple to the wall of the city" to make it a place of refuge.

---

[13]Herodotus, *The History of Herodotus*, vol. 1, trans. G. C. Macaulay (New York: MacMillan, 1890).

Euripides, ca. 480–ca. 406 BCE

Hippolytus 9-30:[14] Aphrodite tells how an Amazonian woman had a celibate son, Hippolytus. He turned his back "on any thought of marriage" and worshiped Artemis, "believing her to be the greatest god of all." They hunted together with their dogs. But Aphrodite saw their "close relationship" as "too close for any mortal with a god." And since she perceived that Hippolytus slighted her in favoring Artemis, Aphrodite determined, "today I will avenge myself on him."

Notice that although Artemis's companions are usually women, she does not despise celibate men: Hippolytus says, "Sing of heavenly Artemis, great Zeus's child and our protector!" At her statue, he presents a garland of woven flowers, saying, "These flowers the virtuous may pick, the ones who keep a constant rein on their desires in all they do, whose virtue comes from who they are and not from what they have been taught. But those who are not pure may not do so." He takes a step toward the statue and says, "Dear mistress, accept from my chaste hand this flowery wreath for your golden hair. Of mortal men I am the only one who has the privilege of spending time alone with you. We converse together, and though I never gaze upon your face, I can hear your voice. I pray my life will end like this, just as it has begun."

Euripides's chorus describes women in unflattering terms, identifying their most vulnerable time as childbirth. But he notes that Artemis delivers laboring women as a midwife with power to ease all labor pains:

> But women's nature tends to show
> a lack of balance—in childbirth
> a sense of wretched helplessness
> combined with utter folly.
> Those feelings pierce my womb, as well,
> but I call out to Artemis,
> guardian goddess of the bow,

---

[14]Euripides, *Hippolytus*, trans. Ian Johnston (2020), http://johnstoniatexts.x10host.com/euripides/hippolytushtml.html.

who eases all our labor pains.
She never fails to visit me—
gods be thanked—and is most welcome!

As Euripides's story continues, once Aphrodite has taken revenge on Hippolytus, Artemis expresses to his father her distain for Aphrodite, whom Artemis says that "those of us who prize virginity" consider "the enemy we find most hateful."

Artemis is, in the words of S. M. Baugh, "the ever-virgin consort of wild forest nymphs, who spurned marriage and relations with men. Her devotees, like priggish Hippolytus, were distinguished by perfect chastity."[15]

Plato, ca. 427–347 BCE

From Plato we see affirmation of a recurring theme of Artemis and sex—that is, the absence of it. Plato says the goddess is sound/healthy, loves virginity, and her very name may be rooted in her hating sexual intercourse:

Cratylus 406.B:[16] "Artemis appears to get her name from her healthy [*artemes*] and well-ordered nature, and her love of virginity; or perhaps he who named her meant that she is learned in virtue or possibly, too, that she hates sexual intercourse [*aroton misei*] of man and woman; or he who gave the goddess her name may have given it for any or all of these reasons."

Callimachus, ca. 305–ca. 240 BCE

Hymn 3.1-45:[17] Callimachus begins with a veiled hint of Artemis's volatility: "No light thing is it for singers to forget her." He is doubtless referring to Oeneus, whom Homer described bringing firstfruit offerings to all the gods except Artemis and paying for it. Callimachus

---

[15]S. M. Baugh, "A Foreign World: Ephesus in the First Century," in *Women in the Church: An Analysis and Application of 1 Timothy 2:9-15*, 2nd ed., ed. Andreas J. Köstenberger and Thomas R. Schreiner (Grand Rapids, MI: Baker Academic, 2005), 50.

[16]Plato, *Plato in Twelve Volumes*, vol. 12, trans. Harold N. Fowler, Loeb Classical Library (Cambridge, MA: Harvard University Press, 1921).

[17]Callimachus, *Works*, trans. A. W. Mair (London: William Heinemann, 1921), *Hymn* 3.1-45.

describes Artemis as one "whose study is the bow and the shooting of hares and the spacious dance and sport upon the mountains."

As a girl on her father's knee, Artemis makes big requests. Her first is, "Give me to keep my virginity, Father, forever." She's consistent on this point. Next, she asks that she might have many names. She also wants a bow but not a quiver because Cyclopes can make one for her. Rather, she wants to be "bringer of light."

As to apparel, she asks for "a tunic with embroidered border reaching to the knee"—the length short so that she "may slay wild beasts."

Next, she wants "sixty daughters of Oceanus for my choir—all nine years old, all maidens yet ungirdled" to tend her calf-high boots and take care of her hounds after she hunts.

While her father might be prepared to give her cities, Artemis asks for all the mountains. She concedes that her father may allot her whatever cities he likes, but she explains:

> The cities of men I will visit only when women vexed by the sharp pang of childbirth call me to their aid. Even in the hour when I was born, the Fates ordained that I should be their helper, forasmuch as my mother suffered no pain either when she gave me birth or when she carried me within her womb, but without travail put me from her body.

Here Zeus vows to give Artemis even more than requested—promising that thirty cities will glorify only Artemis, whom he says will watch over streets and harbors. Having received her wish, Artemis departs for Crete to choose her nine-year-old nymphs. The parents of the virgin daughters sent to attend Artemis are proud to offer them to her.

Putting this all together, one can see the rationale for Artemis being a goddess of midwifery while also being a virgin in the strictest sense. She is not a mother or a nurturer or a fertility goddess. She is a virgin goddess specializing in several things, including painless delivery or painless deaths, especially related to childbearing.

In another hymn, Callimachus describes the goddess as "Slayer of Tityus":

Hymn 3.110-12:[18] "Artemis, Lady of Maidenhood, Slayer of Tityus, golden were your arms and golden your belt, and a golden car did you yoke, and golden bridles, goddess, did you put on your deer."

(*Trigger warning*: sexual violence.)

According to Pindar (ca. 518–ca. 437 BCE),[19] the story went something like this: the giant Tityus tried to sexually assault Artemis's mother when she passed through his region. Her twins rushed to their mother's aid and slew the giant with their darts, dispatching him to Hades for torment. The way Pindar describes it, Lord Artemis hunted him down with arrows from her unconquerable quiver. In his reference to Artemis as "lord," Callimachus uses *kyria*, the female counterpart to "lord."[20] Here we have *maidenhood* versus *matronhood*. Artemis is the lord of virginity, who wears a gold belt, drives a golden chariot, and sits on a golden throne. Not only arrows but darts proceed from her bow. One wonders if the apostle Paul's reference to the enemy's "flaming arrows" in Ephesians 6:16, mentioned in a context of spiritual warfare (Eph 6:10-18), might carry a veiled reference to a specific enemy he has in view. The antidote he proposes for extinguishing flaming arrows is to armor oneself with the shield of faith.

In another of Callimachus's hymns, Artemis bears a silver bow instead of a gold one. Her shooting has a progression:

---

[18]Callimachus, *Works*, *Hymn* 3.110-12.

[19]Pindar, "Pythian 4," 4.4 in *Pythian Odes*, trans. Diane Arnson Svarlien, 1990, www.perseus.tufts.edu /hopper/text?doc=Perseus%3Atext%3A1999.01.0162%3Abook%3DP.%3Apoem%3D4, accessed February 27, 2023.

[20]Hereafter I will translate *kyria* as "lord." The title attributed to Artemis appears with either masculine or feminine endings. Also, Oxford Languages lists the primary meaning of *lady* in English as "a woman," https://tinyurl.com/2p93c2d5 (accessed February 27, 2023) and its second entry, *mistress*, is "a woman having an extramarital sexual relationship, especially with a married man" https://tinyurl .com/2495f6xh, (accessed February 27, 2023). So *lord* captures the sense better. Oster follows this practice of translation: Richard Oster, "Ephesus as a Religious Center under the Principate, I. Paganism before Constantine," in *Aufstieg und Niedergang der Römischen Welt*, ed. Wolfgang Haase and Hildegard Temporini (New York: Walter de Gruyter, 1990), 1724.

Hymn 3.115-28:[21] "First at an elm, and next at an oak" and third "a wild beast." But the fourth time she "shot at the city of unjust men . . . forward men" on whom she will impress her "grievous wrath." Note what makes men unjust here: they "missed the mark" not only against each other but against strangers—thus incurring Artemis's wrath. Such wrath takes several forms that reveal her ruthlessness: "Plague feeds on their cattle; frost feeds on their tilth; the old men cut their hair in mourning over their sons"—that is, fathers mourn dead sons—"and their wives either are smitten or die in childbirth. If they escape, they bear birds, whereof none stands on upright ankle." Even those who do escape have birds who cannot even stand up straight. Artemis's wrath is fierce. Notice the connection again to midwifery but not mothering or nurturing. This goddess kills more women than men, yet she protects midwives. She despises the gaze and touch of men, but she does not dislike men.

Artemis's hunting companions and fellow female hunters are described:

Hymn 3.204-20:[22] First is Cyrene, a maiden daughter who guarded her father's herds, slaying wild beasts with javelin and sword. Next is "the fair-haired wife of Cephalus" whom "Lord Artemis made a fellow in the chase," and after her is "fair Anticleia," beloved by the goddess. Speaking to Artemis, the author writes, "These were the first who wore the gallant bow and arrow-holding quivers on their shoulders; their right shoulders bore the quiver strap, and always the right breast showed bare." One wonders if the description commonly attributed to the Amazon women, that of having one bare breast (they were also rendered this way on some ancient statues), might be rooted in Callimachus's description of Artemis's band of female archers.

In Greek mythology, Proetus was king of Argos. He had three daughters who were driven mad either because they had insulted

---

[21]Callimachus, *Works*, Hymn 3.115-28.
[22]Callimachus, *Works*, *Hymn to Artemis* 3.204-20.

Hera or because they refused to accept the new rites of Dionysus. In their madness, they believed themselves to be cows, wandering the land and mooing. In one version of this tale,[23] the daughters recover when Proetus prays to Artemis. Notice how an Artemis shrine assigns her a surname here, "Artemis of Virginity," in connection with this specific event. Artemis has numerous surnames, including "of the Ephesians."

Hymn 3.233-55:[24]

> For you [Artemis] surely Proetus established two shrines, one of Artemis of Virginity for that you did gather for him his virgin daughters when they were wandering over the Azanian hills; the other he founded in Lusa to Artemis the Gentle, because you took from his daughters the spirit of wildness. For you, too, the Amazons, whose mind is set on war, in Ephesus beside the sea, established an image beneath an oak trunk, and Hippo performed a holy rite for you, and they themselves, O Upis[25] Queen, around the image danced a war-dance—first in shields and armor, and again in a circle arraying a spacious choir . . . for your shafts are ever more set as a defense before Ephesus.

Notice here the links between Artemis, the Amazons, and Ephesus. Apparently, the Amazons established an image (the first?) to Artemis in Ephesus behind an oak trunk. "Hippo" is likely a shortening of Hippolyta, queen of the Amazons. She led the holy rite for Artemis and the Amazons, dancing a war dance with shields and armor. Note also the connection between Artemis and the defense of Ephesus.

Hymn to Artemis 3.259-68:[26] Callimachus, in his hymn to Artemis, exhorts, "Let none disparage Artemis. O Lord of Munychia, Watcher of Harbors, hail, Lord of Pherae! For Oeneus dishonored her altar and

---

[23]"To her once the son of Abas and his daughters with beautiful robes set up an altar where many prayers are offered." Bacchylides, *Odes*, trans. Diane Arnson Svarlien, (1991), 11, www.perseus.tufts .edu/hopper/text?doc=Perseus%3Atext%3A1999.01.0064%3Abook%3DEp%3Apoem%3D11.

[24]Callimachus, *Works*, *Hymn to Artemis* 3.233-55.

[25]*Upis* is one of Artemis's many names.

[26]Callimachus, *Works*, *Hymn to Artemis* 3.259-68.

no pleasant struggles came upon his city. Nor let any contend with her in shooting of stags or in archery."

The author is naming powerful men who crossed Artemis and suffered for their actions. Recall that Oeneus neglected to sacrifice to her the first fruits of his harvest, so she sent a wild boar to ravage his land: "For the son of Atreus vaunted him not that he suffered small requital." He continues, "Neither let any woo the virgin; for not Otus, nor Orion wooed her to their own good. Nor let any shun the yearly dance; for not tearless to Hippo was her refusal to dance around the altar. Hail, great queen, and graciously greet my song."

Elsewhere, one learns that the son of Atreus—that is, Agamemnon—led the Greek fleet bound for Troy. On his way to the Trojan War, as the story goes, he killed a stag on Artemis's sacred ground and had the gall to brag about it. The outraged goddess retaliated by sending stormy gales that prevented Agamemnon and his troops from sailing until he sacrificed his daughter, Iphigenia; Artemis then relented. The sacrifice of Iphigenia is not explicitly mentioned by Homer, but it appears in several other authors.[27]

(*Trigger warning*: Sexual violence mentioned.)

Another man mentioned in this passage by Callimachus is Otus, one of Poseidon's twin sons. He and his brother grew into giants and became invincible—and thus arrogant. One desired to violate Hera, but Otus wanted to rape Artemis. On their way to take over the world, the twins locked Ares in a bronze jar. During a break from battle, they called repeatedly for Hera and Artemis. After the goddesses refused, Artemis finally went to Otus and told him he could have his way with her if he would free Ares. Otus was ecstatic, but his brother was angry, so the two quarreled. While they were distracted, Artemis turned into a deer and sprang between them. Both men threw

---

[27]In Aeschylus's *Agamemnon*, the sacrifice of Iphigenia is motivation for a plot to murder Agamemnon. In some versions, such as Hyginus's *Fabulae*, Iphigenia is not sacrificed at all. The Hesiodic *Catalogue of Women* has Artemis transforming her into the goddess Hecate.

spears at the creature, but she was so fast that they missed her and impaled each other.

Additionally, Callimachus mentions Orion. He and Artemis were companions who hunted together, constantly seeking to outdo each other. But when Orion boasted to Artemis that he could slay anything that came from the earth, Gaia, who considered all living things on earth her children, sought revenge. She summoned a giant scorpion that Artemis and Orion had to fight together. Orion was killed during this battle—possibly from the scorpion's sting, perhaps from Artemis's accidental arrow. (Callimachus seems to view it as the latter.) At the request of heartbroken Artemis, the fallen hunter was placed in the sky as the constellation Orion along with the scorpion as Scorpio.

As to the identity of the Hippo who refused to dance around the altar, she is perhaps the same Hippo who led the dance for Artemis in Ephesus. Classics scholar Martin Robertson notes that this latter story is not developed in any other source. Some think Hippo refused to dance because she broke her vow of chastity and was killed by Artemis.[28]

Conclusions from literary sources in antiquity. A survey of these ancient sources reveals consistent themes in stories about and many titles of Artemis. She is the daughter of Zeus and Leto, the twin of Apollo, and a lover of archery and game hunting. Artemis is associated with loveliness, gold, beautiful apparel, Amazons, and Ephesus. She is also volatile, known to be vengeful against those who slight her. She kills a lot, though she can make death pain free.

As for Artemis's relationship with males, Lilly Nortjé-Meyer observes:

> The only man Artemis had romantic feelings for was Orion. After his death she never loved another man. It does not speak of a promiscuous goddess, but of a strong woman who allowed herself to experience true love, but not be dependent on the love of a man. The high value Artemis

---

[28]Martin Robertson, *The Eye of Greece: Studies in the Art of Athens* (Cambridge: Cambridge University Press, 1982), 86.

placed on virginity should be seen not only as the absence of sexual relations, but rather as the completeness of her female identity. She did not need a man; she could be complete without male companionship.[29]

Michael Immendörfer notes,

Artemis killed Ariadne, the daughters of Niobe, the mothers of Sarpedon and Andromache and the wife of Eumaios. She [Artemis] cooperates, in part, with her twin brother, Apollo. While he kills men, Artemis is the goddess of death, especially for women. She kills from a distance, suddenly, without illness, and sometimes gently, but also in anger.[30]

Artemis's father, Zeus, granted her wish to make her a perpetual virgin. Although she rarely consorts with men and does kill a lot of women, Artemis is also the one on whom those in labor call when they need a midwife. They expect her either to deliver them safely or kill them painlessly.

Nortjé-Meyer offers a rationale for how Artemis came to be so associated with midwifery:

Artemis's experience of her mother's suffering during the birth of her brother Apollo negatively influenced her view of childbearing and marriage in such a way that she never wanted to have her own children; she developed an aversion to marriage and was known as the eternal virgin goddess. She became the protector of women giving birth and of young children.[31]

As for the goddess's virginity, Nortjé-Meyer explains, "Artemis was sacred about her privacy, freedom, and nudity, something that is reflected in the clothing donations she received from her devotees as

---

[29]Lilly (SJ) Nortjé-Meyer and Alta Vrey, "Artemis as Matrix for a New Interpretation of the Household Codes in Ephesians 5:22-6:9," *Neotestamentica* 50, no. 1 (2016): 63.

[30]Michael Immendörfer, *Ephesians and Artemis: The Cult of the Great Goddess of Ephesus as the Epistle's Context*, Wissenschaftliche Untersuchungen zum Neuen Testament II 436 (Tübingen: Mohr Siebeck, 2017), 224.

[31]L. Nortjé-Meyer, "Die hiërargiese funksionering van God, mans en vroue in die brief aan die Efersiërs," *Verbum et Ecclesia* 21, no. 1 (2003): 188.

offerings."[32] Nortjé-Meyer notes the seeming inconsistences relating to Artemis and delivery: "She was not simple and easy to understand, but complex. She was worshipped as the goddess who protects women during childbirth, but could also cause their death with her arrows. Like her brother Apollo she was the goddess of healing, but she could also spread diseases."[33]

Being a midwife was an important job in a world in which women were pressured to bear children and in which they faced more risk of early death than "even the most afflicted country in the modern world."[34]

In *The Body and Society*, Peter Brown places the empire-wide life expectancy at the time of the earliest Christians at less than twenty-five years. "Of those surviving childhood," he says, "only four out of every hundred men, and fewer women, lived beyond age fifty." What that meant for the average matron: to maintain zero population growth, each wife had to produce an average of five children.[35] And these women started early. As Baugh notes, "Greek women were married between age 14 or 15 and men around age 30."[36] Then, much more than now, a primary concern of women was surviving childbirth.

WRITERS FROM THE FIRST CENTURIES

Having established a description of Artemis drawn from sources in antiquity, we determine next which of these characteristics continued through the first centuries BCE and CE. Identifying the Ephesian version of Artemis at the time of the earliest Christians requires a look at literary sources roughly contemporary with Paul and Timothy that also describe Artemis of Ephesus.

---

[32]Nortjé-Meyer, "Die hiërargiese," 188.

[33]Nortjé-Meyer and Vrey, "Artemis," 63.

[34]Peter Brown, *The Body and Society: Men, Women, and Sexual Renunciation in Early Christianity* (New York: Columbia University Press, 1988), 6.

[35]Brown, *The Body*, 6.

[36]S. M. Baugh, "Cult Prostitution in New Testament Ephesus: A Reappraisal," *Journal of the Evangelical Theological Society* 42, no. 3 (September 1999): 449; citing Sarah Pomeroy, *Families in Classical and Hellenistic Greece: Representations and Realities* (Oxford: Clarendon, 1996), 5-7.

The author of the book of Acts said that the people chanted "Great is Artemis *of the Ephesians*" (Acts 19:28, 34, emphasis mine). Most Ephesus scholars, including historians and religious experts, seem to differentiate between the Ephesian manifestation of the goddess and the more generic Artemis. Trebilco says that although Artemis of Ephesus is similar to Artemis of the Greeks, there were substantial differences between the two.[37]

How do the manifestations differ? In appearance—as we will see in statues and coins. But why the same name? What qualities did they share? Ancient gods and goddesses sometimes took on distinct personas in different cities. Artemis of antiquity and Artemis of the Ephesians share the same backstory, but they have differing emphases. Consider modern parallels: "The Statue of Liberty Enlightening the World" in New York harbor has a connection with immigration and huddled masses that the same Statue of Liberty in Paris lacks. In Nazareth's Church of the Annunciation, one can see numerous depictions of Madonna and child, including Jesus and Mary as Bolivian, Mexican, and Japanese.

As for titles, Our Lady of Guadalupe is still Jesus' mother, but her title is location specific and connected with a local narrative. The Black Madonna of Częstochowa, the Virgin of Candelaria, and Our Lady of Ferguson are all names given to Jesus' mother along with local narratives.

We will begin by looking at sources roughly contemporary with the New Testament. We first look at writings about the goddess that do not necessarily connect Artemis with Ephesus, followed by those that do.

Strabo, ca. 64 BCE–23 CE

The Greek geographer, philosopher, and historian Strabo lived in Asia Minor. He provides a birth narrative of Artemis that competes with the Ephesian version. This version names Apollo first and places the births of both twins in Delos.

---

[37]Paul Trebilco, *The Early Christians in Ephesus from Paul to Ignatius* (Grand Rapids, MI: Eerdmans, 2007), 19.

Geography 10.5.2:[38]

Now, the city which belongs to Delos, as also the temple of Apollo. . . . From olden times, beginning with the times of the heroes, Delos has been revered because of its gods, for the myth is told that there Leto was delivered of her travail by the birth of Apollo and Artemis: "For aforetime," says Pindar, "it was tossed by the billows, by the blasts of all manner of winds, but when the daughter of Coeüs [Leto] in the frenzied pangs of childbirth set foot upon it, then did four pillars, resting on adamant, rise perpendicular from the roots of the earth, and on their capitals sustain the rock. And there she gave birth to, and beheld, her blessed offspring." The neighboring islands, called the Cyclades, made it famous, since in its honor they would send at public expense sacred envoys, sacrifices, and choruses composed of virgins, and would celebrate great general festivals there.

Compare this with what Strabo writes later, again mentioning Apollo first when speaking of the twins.

Geography 14.1.6:[39] "Apollo is the god of healing. And Artemis has her name from the fact that she makes people 'Artemeas,' or sound. And both Helius and Selenê are closely associated with these, since they are the causes of the temperature of the air. And both pestilential diseases and sudden deaths are imputed to these gods."

Strabo uses the modifier *sound* not in the sense of hearing but in the sense of being free of injury, disease, or decay. Spencer translates Strabo here as "safe and sound" and notes that Artemidorus adds "healthy."[40] Changes in air temperature, pestilential diseases, and sudden deaths are attributed to the twin gods.

Ovid, 34 BCE–17 CE

Writing in Latin, Ovid uses the Roman names for gods. Here Artemis is Diana; Zeus is Jupiter/Jove; and Zeus's wife, Hera, is Juno.

[38] Strabo, *Geography*, trans. Horace L. Jones, Loeb Classical Library (Cambridge, MA: Harvard University Press, 1924), 10.2.

[39] Strabo, *Geography*, 14.1.6.

[40] Aída Besançon Spencer, *1 Timothy*, New Covenant Commentary Series (Eugene, OR: Cascade Books, 2013), 21.

Callisto is one of Artemis's hunting companions, who has sworn to remain a virgin.

(*Trigger warning*: Nudity, sexual violence implied.)

Metamorphoses 2.417-65:[41]

The sun was high, just path [*sic*] the zenith, when she [Callisto] entered a grove that had been untouched through the years. Here she took her quiver from her shoulder, unstrung her curved bow, and lay down on the grass, her head resting on her painted quiver. Jupiter, seeing her there weary and unprotected, said, "Here, surely, my wife will not see my cunning, or if she does find out it is, oh it is, worth a quarrel!" Quickly he took on the face and dress of Diana, and said "Oh, girl who follows me, where in my domains have you been hunting?"

The virgin girl got up from the turf replying, "Greetings, goddess greater than Jupiter: I say it even though he himself hears it." He did hear, and laughed, happy to be judged greater than himself, and gave her kisses unrestrainedly, and not those that virgins give. When she started to say in which woods she had hunted, he embraced and prevented her—and not without committing a crime. Face to face with him, as far as a woman could, (I wish you had seen her, Juno: you would have been kinder to her) she fought him. But how could a girl win, and who is more powerful than Jove? Victorious, Jupiter made for the furthest reaches of the sky: while to Callisto the grove was odious, and the wood seemed knowing. As she retraced her steps, she almost forgot her quiver and its arrows, and the bow she had left hanging.

Diana and her band of female hunters approach and, upon seeing Callisto, call out to her. But she runs away, worried that Diana is Jupiter in disguise again. But when Callisto sees the other nymphs, she relaxes and joins their number.

Sometime later, Diana is faint from the chase in Apollo's hot sunlight and finds a grove with a stream winding over sand. She tests the

---

[41]Ovid, *Metamorphoses*, trans. A. S. Kline (2000), 2.417-65. www.poetryintranslation.com/PITBR /Latin/Metamorph2.php#anchor_Toc64106117.

water with her foot and says, "Any witness is far away. Let's bathe our bodies naked in the flowing water."

Callisto tries to avoid undressing, but she cannot conceal her swollen belly. Upon seeing it, the goddess cries out, "Go, far away from here. Do not pollute the sacred fountain!" and commands her to leave her band of followers.

From Diana's point of view, even victims of sexual assault are polluters, guilty for having lost their virginity. This story illustrates how highly the hunting moon goddess values virginity and how ruthless she is about it. Notice in Ovid's next narrative a similar response to nudity in mixed company.

(*Trigger warning*: Nudity.)

Metamorphoses 3.150-205:[42] As Ovid tells it, virgin Artemis of the high-girded tunic has a favorite sacred cave where she bathes. Having reached the place, she gives her spear, quiver, and unstrung bow to her weapon-bearer, a nymph. Another holds her robe, while two unfasten her sandals. Another loosens her hair as five more nymphs draw water and pour it over her.

While she is bathing, Actaeon innocently enters the sacred grove. He and the naked nymphs see each other, and they beat at their breasts, "filling the whole wood with their sudden outcry." They rush to surround Diana to hide her with their bodies. But the goddess stands head and shoulders above them all. Diana's face turns "the color of clouds stained by the opposing shafts of sun, or Aurora's brightness."

Artemis looks around, wishing she had her arrows. She scoops up a handful of water and throws it in Actaeon's face. She turns him into a mature stag, lengthening his neck and making his ear-tips pointed. She changes feet for hands, long legs for arms, and covers his body with a dappled hide. Finally, she adds fear.

---

[42]Ovid, *Metamorphoses*, trans. A. S. Kline (2000), 3.150-205, www.poetryintranslation.com/PITBR /Latin/Metamorph3.php#anchor_Toc64106183.

He flies off marveling at his own swift speed. "But when he saw his head and horns reflected in the water, he tried to say 'Oh, look at me!' But no voice followed. He groaned: that was his voice, and tears run down his altered face. Only his mind remained unchanged."

Although Actaeon's entry on the scene happens innocently, Artemis is ruthless about chastity. One sees consistency historically. In Baugh's words, "Artemis was repelled by sexual contact of any kind."[43]

Having considered these stories from the first century that do not connect Artemis with Ephesus, we turn to those that do.

Strabo, ca. 64 BCE–23 CE

Strabo gives the most detailed account connecting Artemis's birth with Ephesus, even though he places Artemis and Apollo's birth event elsewhere, in Delos. He has begun by describing the approach to Ephesus by sea to the harbor called Panormus with the temple of Artemis.

Geography 14.1.20:

On the same coast, slightly above the sea, is also Ortygia, which is a magnificent grove of all kinds of trees, of the cypress most of all. It is traversed by the Cenchrius River, where Leto is said to have bathed herself after her travail.[44] For here is the mythical scene of the birth, and of the nurse Ortygia, and of the holy place where the birth took place, and of the olive tree nearby, where the goddess [Leto] is said first to have taken a rest after she was relieved from her travail . . . There are several temples in the place, some ancient and others built in later times; and in the ancient temples are many ancient wooden images, but in those of later times there are works of Scopas; for example, Leto holding a scepter and Ortygia standing beside her with a child in each arm. A general festival is held there annually; and by a certain custom the youths vie for honor, particularly in the splendor of their banquets there. At that time, also, a

---

[43]Baugh, "Cult Prostitution," 458.
[44]That is, in delivering her twins, Artemis and Apollo.

special college of the Curetes[45] holds symposiums and performs certain mystic sacrifices.[46]

The Ortygia mentioned above does double duty as the name of both Leto's midwife and the olive grove where Leto recovered from her travail. In this account, both Artemis and Apollo are born near Ephesus. The wooden images of brother and sister are said to be depicted in a temple image in which their nurse holds one twin on each of her arms.

Strabo references an annual festival in Ephesus, which he connects with the natal story. He mentions a college of Curetes—which other sources, both literary and epigraphic, suggest are an important part of the cult of Artemis. One can see how a link between Artemis's birthplace, attendance at her brother's difficult birth, the goddess's reputation for deliverance, and the well-documented annual celebration of her birthday in Ephesus would reinforce Artemis's connection both with the city and childbirth.

Tacitus, ca. 56–120 CE

Tacitus acknowledges the two narratives of Artemis and Apollo's birth event, but he discounts the version placing their natal story in Delos, calling it "common" and favoring the Ephesian version.

The Annals 3.61:[47]

> The people of Ephesus . . . declared that Artemis and Apollo were not born at Delos, as was the vulgar belief. They had in their own country a river Cenchrius, a grove Ortygia, where Leto, as she leaned in the pangs of labor on an olive [tree] still standing, gave birth to those two deities, whereupon the grove at the divine intimation was consecrated.

---

[45] The Curetes, male equivalent of Nymphs, were young divine warriors from Crete. "Their role here parallels what they did at the birth of Zeus, when they made a great deal of noise to frighten off his father Cronus, who was accustomed to swallowing his children immediately after their birth (Strabo 10.3.11). Without the willingness of the Curetes to take up arms Artemis would not have been born near Ephesus." Jerome Murphy-O'Connor, *St. Paul's Ephesus: Texts and Archaeology* (Collegeville, MN: Liturgical Press, 2008), 16.

[46] Strabo, *Geography*, 14.1.20.

[47] Cornelius Tacitus, *Annales ab excessu divi Augusti*, trans. Charles Dennis Fisher (Oxford: Clarendon Press, 1906).

There Apollo himself . . . pardoned the suppliant Amazons who had gathered round the shrine. Subsequently by the permission of Hercules, when he was subduing Lydia, the grandeur of the temple's ceremony was augmented, and during the Persian rule its privileges were not curtailed.

Like Strabo, Tacitus notes the existence of a grove called *Ortygia*, consecrated as the sacred birthplace. Tacitus aligns with the more ancient authors linking Artemis and Ephesus with the Amazons, as he locates the pardoning of the Amazons here. These female warriors apparently gathered at the shrine marking the twins' birthplace. The temple which he associates with ceremony, grandeur, and privilege is that of Artemis in Ephesus.

Pausanias, 110–180 CE

The ten-volume *Description of Greece* by the geographer Pausanias, the most important literary source relating to Artemis Ephesia outside of the book of Acts, dates to the second century CE. Pausanias traveled throughout the Roman Empire describing what he saw, often giving the history of contemporary practices. While his work includes many references to the goddess Artemis with no titles, it also contains numerous references to Artemis of the Ephesians. In fact, the goddess's most popular surname in his records, even outside of Ephesus, was *of the Ephesians*. A glance at the modern index to Pausanias's complete works reveals many single references to Artemis with different surnames in various places, but the entry for *Artemis of the Ephesians* goes on for five lines of index entries.

In W. H. S. Jones's introduction to Pausanias's first volume, the translator writes, "Any reader of Pausanias will be struck by the number of epithets or surnames attached to the names of certain gods. What follows is a list of the chief deities he mentions with the number of surnames given to each."[48] Rearranged here in order of frequency, his list shows that Artemis was second only to Zeus in her renown:

---

[48]Pausanias, *Description of Greece*, trans. W. H. S. Jones, Loeb Classical Library (Cambridge, MA: Harvard University Press, 1978), 1.xxii-xxv.

- Zeus, 67
- Artemis, 64
- Athena, 59
- Apollo, 58
- Aphrodite, 27
- Dionysus, 27
- Demeter, 26
- Hera, 18
- Poseidon, 18
- Hermes, 15
- Heracles, 11
- Asclepius, 10
- Nymphs, 10
- Core, 6
- Ares, 4
- Pan, 4
- Fortune, 3
- Disocuri, 2
- Muses, 2
- Sleep, 1

Jones explains what he considers the significance of these names and the frequency of their occurrences: "The mere number of epithets attached to a deity is a fair test of the power of his [or her] cult to appeal to the religious instinct."[49] If Jones is right, Artemis was second only to Zeus, and Artemis of the Ephesians was her most common title.

---

[49]Pausanias, *Description*, 1.xxi.

Jones goes on to note that many of the epithets Pausanias cites refer to the city or place in which a cult was established. He lists Artemis as surnamed Brauronian, of the Ephesians, Munychian, and Tauric. Other surnames, he says, are derived from animals. He also notes that many of the epithets refer to some aspect of a deity's power or a characteristic of the god or goddess, or even a way in which one supplanted another, such as Artemis supplanting Dictynna, the goddess of nets. In other cases, Jones writes, "The epithet perpetuates some detail of a legend . . . of a temple . . . or even a type of image."[50] This explains why Pausanias treats the Ephesian Artemis as a variation on the same Artemis found all over Asia, not a different goddess with the same name.

Consistent with what the New Testament reports about the silver-workers' view of Artemis's renown (Acts 19:27), Pausanias says that numerous references to Artemis of the Ephesians appear in cities other than Ephesus—in some cases separated by great distance. He mentions, for example, an image of Artemis of the Ephesians that he saw in Corinth,[51] about 350 miles away. In the same sentence he refers to an image of the god Dionysus with no city attribution or other surname. One might expect Pausanias to have described the Artemis statue in Corinth as simply Artemis with no surname, or as Artemis of Corinth. But the specific *Artemis of the Ephesians* found in Corinth is the Artemis with a uniquely Ephesian persona.

Pausanias's observations also include:

Description of Greece 4.31.8:[52]

> But all cities worship Artemis of Ephesus, and individuals hold her in honor above all the gods. The reason . . . is the renown of the Amazons, who traditionally dedicated the image; also the extreme antiquity of this sanctuary. Three other points as well have contributed to her renown:

---

[50]Pausanias, *Description*, 1.xxii–xxv.
[51]Pausanias, *Description*, 2.2.6.
[52]Pausanias, *Description*, 4.31.8.

the size of the temple—surpassing all buildings among men; the eminence of the city of the Ephesians; and the renown of the goddess who dwells there.

Description of Greece 7.2.7:

Pindar [sixth century BCE] . . . says that this sanctuary [of Artemis] was founded by the Amazons during their campaign against Athens and Theseus. It is a fact that the women from the Thermodon, as they knew the sanctuary from of old, sacrificed to the Ephesian goddess both on this occasion and when they had fled from Heracles; some of them earlier still, when they had fled from Dionysus, having come to the sanctuary as suppliants. However, it was not by the Amazons that the sanctuary was founded, but by Coresus, an aboriginal, and Ephesus, who is thought to have been a son of the river Cayster, and from Ephesus the city received its name.

The inhabitants of the land were partly Leleges, a branch of the Carians, but the greater number were Lydians. In addition, there were others who dwelt around the sanctuary for the sake of its protection, and these included some women of the race of the Amazons.[53]

Pausanias attributes the worldwide worship and honor of Artemis of Ephesus to the Amazons' renown. He notes that the connection between these warriors and their goddess dates to extreme antiquity, with the Amazons making the initial dedication. Artemis's temple in his day was one of the Seven Wonders of the World (considered by many to be the greatest), and the city, eminent. Though he discounts the version of the sanctuary's founding that attributes it to the Amazons, he does acknowledge that women from Thermodon knew of the sanctuary and sacrificed to Artemis there on more than one occasion.

So according to this geographer writing during the era in question, a prevailing belief about Ephesus's history was that the Amazons, while

---

[53]Pausanias, *Description*, 7.2.7.

not the city's founders, had lived around Artemis's temple, there, enjoying protection from its goddess. He presents the Ephesian Artemis
as having a strong connection to the Amazons, whom he treats as historical rather than mythological.

Plutarch, 46–119 CE

Greek gods and goddesses were considered neither omnipotent nor
omnipresent. Therefore, Plutarch acknowledges that the Ephesian Artemis could not be in two places at the same time:

Life of Alexander 3.3:[54]

> Alexander [the Great] was born early in the month Hecatombaeon, the
> Macedonian name for which is Loüs, on the sixth day of the month, and
> on this day the temple of Ephesian Artemis was burned. It was apropos
> of this that Hegesias the Magnesian made an utterance frigid enough to
> have extinguished that great conflagration. He said, namely, it was no
> wonder that the temple of Artemis was burned down, since the goddess
> was busy bringing Alexander into the world.

In the view of Plutarch, some believed Artemis chose midwifery over
protecting her temple—referring to its first manifestation, which
burned in 356 BCE. Because the goddess had to assist at the birth of
Alexander the Great, her absence left her temple vulnerable. Plutarch
cites Hegesias the Magnesian—Magnesia was only eight miles south of
Ephesus—as being cold enough to have distinguished the fire himself
when he blamed the tragedy on Artemis's absence.

Xenophon, first century CE[55]

In his work *Wealth in Ancient Ephesus and the First Letter of Timothy:
Fresh Insights from* Ephesiaca *by Xenophon of Ephesus*, Gary Hoag notes
that while "ancient historians, poets, benefaction inscriptions, numismatic evidence, and other artifacts have shaped our modern

[54]Plutarch, "The Life of Alexander," in *The Parallel Lives*, Loeb Classical Library (Cambridge, MA:
Harvard University Press, 1919).

[55]From Xenophon, *Ephesian History: Or the Love-Adventure of Abrocomas and Anthia*, trans. Mr. Rooke,
2nd ed. (London: J. Millan, 1727), 1.1.

understanding of the social and cultural world of the wealthy in Ephesus in the first century CE," New Testament scholars have largely overlooked another excellent source: an ancient Greek novel ascribed to Xenophon of Ephesus.[56] The work, *Ephesiaca*, has been dated to the first or second century CE,[57] and its descriptions of the Artemis cult at the time provide a wealth of information.

Ephesiaca 1.1.11: "The yearly festival in honor of Artemis was held in Ephesus." As Xenophon sets the scene, an annual festival in honor of Artemis, rooted in ancient tradition, continues to be held. Virgins assist. Attire is rich. Strangers and citizens alike participate. Virgins and young men scope out potential mates. The procession includes holy utensils, as well as hounds and horses—often associated with Artemis—along with hunting accessories. A detail worth noting is that the reenactment has long been, and still is, of Artemis's birth, not of the births of Artemis *and* Apollo. While it has been suggested that Artemis's connection to Amazons makes her anti-male, associated with a "pagan feminine principle" and committed to female empowerment over men,[58] nothing here hints at such connections.

Ephesiaca 1.1.12: The protagonist, Abrocomas, age sixteen, has a love interest, Anthia, age fourteen. In his eyes she surpasses the rest

---

[56]Gary G. Hoag, *Wealth in Ancient Ephesus and the First Letter of Timothy: Fresh Insights from Ephesiaca by Xenophon of Ephesus*, Bulletin for Biblical Research, Supplement II (Winona Lake, IN: Eisenbrauns, 2015), 11.

[57]Hoag, *Wealth*, 11. In my earlier work, I excluded Xenophon's novel because those who dated it after CE 200 caused me to consider it as possibly too late—inching into the third century. But more recent dating has made me reconsider, thanks to Hoag's work. My colleague, New Testament scholar Joe Fantin, in a personal message provided a short summary of the dating, along with his assessment: "Reardon's collections (*Ancient Greek Novels*) dates it (although with a question mark) to the mid-second century (1989, now in a new edition 2008 but the only change is a new forward). Also, the *Oxford Classical Dictionary* dates it at CE 100–150 as far back as in its third edition (1996; followed by the third revised [2003] and 4th [2012]). Even the first edition (1949) suggests a date between CE 117–263 and the second edition (1970) suggests it can be anytime between around CE 100–263. In 1995, O'Sullivan suggested a first-century date (*Xenophon of Ephesus*); however, this seems to be based on his comparison with Chariton's *Callirhoe*. 'I am beginning to get the sense that this opinion is getting more popular but only within the last 10 years or so. I think most still maintain a second-century date.'"

[58]Spencer, *1 Timothy*, 65. Although I disagree with Spencer's finding in this instance, much of her work in 1 Timothy is commendable, especially as it relates to this topic. See my review, Sandra Glahn, "*1 Timothy*: A Review," *Bibliotheca Sacra* 172, no. 686 (Apr–Jun 2015): 248-50.

of the virgins in beauty. In Xenophon's words, "Her golden hair was partly bound up in tresses, but the greatest part of it hung loose and sported in the wind. Her piercing eyes carried mirth, as a virgin, but darted severity, as an emblem of chastity. Her attire was a purple gown, hanging loose from her waist to her knees. The skin of a fawn girded it round, on which hung her quiver and arrows. She bore her hunting arms and javelins, and her hounds followed her." He describes the reaction of the crowd: They "adored her as their goddess; and the multitude viewing her have cried out with amazement, so that there has been a strange confusion of voices, one part affirming her to be Artemis herself, the other, one of her companions." Early in the story, the young man and this Artemis look-alike marry.

The storyteller describes the Ephesian Artemis as the traditional chaste hunter with golden hair and knee-length tunic. Her costume resembles the ancient literary descriptions of Artemis as a maiden hunter with tunic and tresses. Note also the novelist mentions a grove that evokes connections with Artemis's birth story.

In Xenophon's novel, elements of which Shakespeare probably borrowed for *Romeo and Juliet*, the young newlyweds set out from Ephesus on a journey. They offer prayers for a safe voyage to the Ephesian Artemis before sailing. Even though Xenophon does not connect rich apparel specifically with Artemis, he does mention "many rich and different kinds of apparel," a detail that appears in some contexts where Artemis is mentioned (and also in Paul's words to Timothy about expensive clothing, 1 Tim 2:9).

Twice the characters refer to Artemis as their country's goddess, seeing her as having geographic limitations.[59] But she apparently keeps them safe enough to start the voyage home after enduring many perils. Xenophon ends his story this way:

---

[59]Xenophon, *Ephesian History*, 1.1.52, 66.

Ephesiaca 1.1.110:

In a few days they [the young couple] arrived at Ephesus. The whole city
had already heard of their safety and awaited their approach. When they
gained the shore, they immediately, in the same habit they then wore,
entered the temple of Artemis. Many prayers were then offered, many
sacrifices slain, and many gifts presented to the goddess, marked with
inscriptions of what they had done or suffered. These were no sooner
performed than they returned into the city and reared sumptuous monuments for their parents, whom they'd found dead, either by old age, or
anguish of heart.

Because the couple has a relatively happy ending, they offer gifts to
Artemis, commission inscriptions about their experiences, and build
monuments in memory of their parents. The latter details provide hints
about epigraphic practices.

Achilles Tatius, second century CE

Achilles Tatius, a second-century Greco-Roman writer, has only one
surviving work, a romance titled *The Adventures of Leucippe and Clitophon*. As with Xenophon, his words are fiction, but his descriptions
of cult worship provide clues about what his readers might have assumed. For example, one might expect the temple of the virgin goddess
to have allowed only female virgins inside. But in Achilles Tatius's description, both female virgins and men were allowed; only nonvirgin
women were barred on penalty of death, with the lone exception being
use of the temple as a place of refuge. In such a case a female slave was
allowed inside for the purpose of making a legal complaint. The virginity of maidens was solemnly tested in a nearby cave.

Leucippe and Clitophon 7.13:[60]

Now quite near the country house was the temple of Artemis. . . . The
shrine was actually forbidden to free [matrons], but open to men and

---

[60]Achilles Tatius, *The Adventures of Leucippe and Clitophon*, trans. S. Gaselee (New York: G. P. Putnam's
Sons, 2017), 7.13.

virgins. If any other woman entered it, death was the penalty for her
intrusion, unless she were a slave with a legal complaint against her
master: such a one was permitted to come as a suppliant to the goddess
while the magistrates decided the case between her and the master.

Leucippe and Clitophon 8.6-7:[61]

[Pan] made a gift of the whole spot to Artemis, making a compact with
her that it should be entered by no woman no longer a maid. If therefore
any girl is accused of being of doubtful virginity, she is sent by public
decree to the door of the grotto, and the pan-pipes decide the ordeal for
her; she goes in, clad in the proper dress, and the doors are closed behind
her. If she is in reality a virgin, a clear and divine note is heard, either
because there is some breeze in the place which enters the pipes and makes
a musical sound, or possibly because it is Pan himself that is piping: and
after a short time the doors of the grotto open of their own accord, and
out comes the virgin with a wreath of the foliage of the pine upon her head.
But if she has lied about her virginity, the pan-pipes are silent, and a groan
comes forth from the cave instead of a musical sound; the people go away
and leave the woman inside. On the third day after, the virgin priestess of
the spot comes and finds the pan-pipes lying on the ground, but there is
no trace of the woman. It is advisable therefore that you should take most
careful thought as to the position that you are in, and be prudent.

Elsewhere, in a first-century-CE epigram, an additional connection
is made between the Ephesian Artemis and midwifery in a statement
about a mother who died in childbirth. John Hazel identifies it as the
work of orator and poet Zonas, also known as Diodorus of Sardis.[62] He
lived about fifty miles from Ephesus and was a friend of Diodorus the
Younger, to whom the former refers:

These woeful letters of Diodorus's wisdom tell that I was engraven for
one early dead in childbirth, since she perished in bearing a boy; and I

---

[61]Achilles Tatius, *Leucippe and Clitophon*, 8.6-7.
[62]John Hazel, *Who's Who in the Greek World* (New York: Routledge, 2000), 261.

weep to hold Athenais, the comely daughter of Melo, who left grief to the women of Lesbos and her father Jason; but thou, O Artemis, wert busy with thy beast-slaying hounds.[63]

Zonas blames a stillbirth on Artemis's preoccupation with her hounds. He appears to include presiding at births and protection of the mother as part of Artemis's roles.

The book of Ephesians

After looking at Strabo, Ovid, Tacitus, Pausanias, Plutarch, Xenophon, Achilles Tatius, and Zonas, one more first-century literary source begs investigation—the book of Ephesians. One might think no one would doubt that this New Testament book could provide clues about what Ephesus was like at the time of the earliest Christians, being addressed as it was to believers "in Ephesus," presumably at the time of the earliest Christians. Yet some important New Testament manuscripts lack the words *in Ephesus* in the epistle's introduction.[64] Because the rest of the manuscript copies contain these words, and as the epistle has been traditionally referenced as "to the Ephesians," some translations put brackets around or italicize the phrase *in Ephesus* to alert the reader to the textual issue.

The book of Ephesians was possibly intended for circulation to several churches in Asia known to the apostle Paul. Local congregations that passed it around could have added their own cities' names to the greetings. This could explain why the Marcionite canon excludes Ephesians but refers to a letter written to Laodicea. Yet the city of Laodicea was only about one hundred miles on foot by the trade route from Ephesus, and Immendörfer makes a compelling case for seeing Paul's

---

[63]Diodorus of Sardis, *The Greek Anthology III*, xlv, in J. W. Mackail, *Select Epigrams from the Greek Anthology* (London: Longmans, Green, and Co., 1890). The quote appears with eight other works attributed to Diodorus of Sardis in *The Greek Anthology III*, composed of more than four thousand Greek poems dating to the second and first centuries.

[64]The earliest and most important MSS (P46 ℵ* B* 6 1739 [McionTE]) omit "in Ephesus." For Metzger's notes, see Bruce M. Metzger, *A Textual Commentary on the Greek New Testament*, 2nd ed. (Stuttgart, Germany: German Bible Society, 1994), 532.

epistle to the Ephesians as being written specifically to the church in Ephesus:

> The author [of Ephesians] adopts local Artemis terminology and infuses it with new meaning or defines it in relation to Christ, so that cultic terms are said to criticize the cult, i.e., the author uses the language of the cult of Artemis to polemicise against Artemis. The verbal adoption of the terms consists of a fundamental divergence with regard to contents. As readers were familiar with this language, it is very likely that they recognized the author's allusions and could comprehend the intended associations. They consist of direct attacks on the cult and of indirect polemic. As Paul often uses the words and cultural concepts of recipients, it is reasonable to suggest that the use of these words was not random, but deliberate.[65]

Nevertheless, because the book of Ephesians nowhere mentions Artemis by name, it will be excluded in this section on literary sources. We will revisit it in a later chapter, as some terms found in the book of Ephesians have strong connections with the Artemis cult and may help readers better understand terms found in 1 Timothy.

Conclusions from literary sources in the first centuries. Having considered literary mentions of Artemis in the first centuries—both fiction and nonfiction—we can draw conclusions about Artemis from the literary sources, beginning with what Artemis is *not*.

First, Artemis is not associated with prostitution—whether empire wide or specifically in Ephesus. Baugh notes that "neither Strabo, Pliny the Elder, Dio Chrysostom, Pausanias, Xenophon of Ephesus, Achilles Tatius, nor any other ancient author speaks explicitly or even hints at cult prostitution in either the narrow or broad sense in Ephesus of any period."[66] Baugh also reminds readers that prostitution was made a felonious crime by senatorial decree,[67] and it is highly unlikely that

---

[65]Immendörfer, *Ephesians and Artemis*, 314-15.
[66]Baugh, "Cult Prostitution," 449.
[67]Baugh, "Cult Prostitution," 449, citing Tacitus, *Ann.* 2.85.

temple practice in a cult associated with the very identity of the city would flagrantly violate civil law.

Second, although anti-sex, Artemis is not anti-male. She loved Orion, has plenty of male followers, and is never presented as disliking males.

Third, Artemis is not associated with mothering. She is not a mother, and she does not mother or nurture others. Artemis is not associated with human fertility; she is not a fertility goddess. The survey here reveals nothing to link Artemis with such characteristics. So who is she?

First, Artemis is so associated with chastity and virginity that one could say virginity is her most prominent characteristic.

Second, Artemis is a midwife. She can deliver safely; she also has the power—with gentle arrows—to euthanize, killing painlessly.[68] But she also had the power to allow her own mother to deliver her without pain. As a midwife who helps with delivery, Artemis herself is never seen as the one giving birth, nursing, or caring for a child.

Third, Artemis has a connection with the Amazons. Like them, she is unmarried and wields a weapon.

Fourth, Artemis was born first in the Ephesian version of her birth story.

The literary sources roughly contemporary with the earliest Christians reflect an acceptance of the same story the ancient writers told about Artemis—down to her virginity, her physical description, her

---

[68]See also Annette Weissenrieder, "What Does σωθήσεθαι [*sic*] δὲ διὰ τῆς τεκνογονίας 'to Be Saved by Childbearing' Mean (1 Timothy 2:15)? Insights from Ancient Medical and Philosophical Texts," *Early Christianity* 5 (2014): 313-36. While the author does not differentiate between Artemis and Artemis of the Ephesians, she reaches the same conclusions about Artemis's connection with midwifery being unconnected with sex and/or fertility. She also makes a good case for *childbearing* differing from *child rearing*. For the rest of her argument, however, she relies heavily on fourth- and fifth-century BCE documents as well as an Ephesian physician from the second century CE, but nothing in between; her research spans six centuries of data without establishing what people in first-century Ephesus actually thought. She also says that the writer of 1 Timothy commands women to stay safe and healthy (334), when, in fact, his only command is to let them learn (1 Tim 2:11). With these reservations in mind, I commend the work.

connection with the Amazons, her responsibility for midwifery, and her responsibility for sudden deaths.

Both S. M. Baugh and Richard Oster, eminent Ephesus scholars, reject any fertility associations with Artemis Ephesia because of what they observe as a compelling silence from all the primary sources. With them, we have also found none of the literary descriptions of Artemis to support such an assertion.[69] The burden of proof is on those who would argue otherwise. Artemis is nobody's mother.

---

[69]Baugh, "A Foreign World," 24; Oster, "Ephesus as Religious Center," 1726.

4

ARTEMIS IN THE
EPIGRAPHIC SOURCES

INSCRIPTIONS, ESPECIALLY THOSE RELATING to Ephesus, have
been underutilized in biblical studies.[1] Thirty years ago, when Ephesus
boasted only 3,750 published Greek inscriptions (as of the writing of
this book, the count is closer to 6,000), that number was still the largest
from any city in antiquity apart from Athens, Rome, and possibly Delphi.
Horsley noted that the quantity of texts from this one location alone
qualified Ephesus as special, representative of a large Greco-Roman city.[2]
He encouraged those working in New Testament texts to use them:

> In view of the quantity of inscriptions and papyri being newly published
> each year, nonliterary texts now form (with archaeological finds of other
> kinds) a defacto cutting edge of Classical Studies, even though they have

---

[1] G. H. R. Horsley, in "The Inscriptions of Ephesos and the New Testament," *Novum Testamentum* 34,
no. 2 (April 1992): 105-68, writes about the tendency to focus only on papyri, "which receive consider-
ably more notice in NT circles than inscriptions do." He describes MM's work, *The Vocabulary of the
Greek Testament*, as having tacitly had the effect "of persuading its users that the papyri have far more
to offer than epigraphical material. Furthermore, since the appearance of their dictionary in 1930—a
dictionary which was already nearly a generation out of date by the time it was complete due to the
procedure adopted of publishing in fascicules—the point seems to have become very largely accepted
that the documentary evidence has yielded as much as it is likely to for NT work" (163). He adds that
"at the very least inscriptions, specifically those in Ephesus, can add to our understanding both of the
NT and its multifaceted social environment with which the Christian movement began to interact
within its first few generations" (166). He notes that considering epigraphic evidence "new texts are
being addressed, which in turn so often allow us to view old questions in a new light" (168).

[2] Horsley, "Inscriptions," 121. Beyond Ephesus, Horsley notes the ramifications for NT work: "1625
words occurring in the NT vocabulary are also found in the *IEph.* volumes. This figure (1625/6170) is
slightly more than 25% of the total NT vocabulary represented it the inscriptions of this one city. As
for the proper nouns in the NT which are also present in the Ephesian inscriptions, the percentage
is a little less than one-third (190/670)" (159).

usually been treated as somewhat marginal in comparison with the
dominant position accorded to the honoured legacy of literary works. It
would be a great misfortune if the continuing flow of rich, new documentary evidence about the Graeco-Roman world passes NT researchers
by without their making a concerted effort to draw that material into
their own ambit and to assess its worth for the discipline. . . . But the
danger really lies, I suggest, in another quarter: the tacit acceptance by
so many in the NT field that the contribution which these texts may
make is so minute that they do not really warrant much attention.[3]

Inscriptions are unmediated primary sources from the past—no
scribes have written comments in their margins or edited them.
Available in vast numbers and often in their original contexts, inscriptions can aid interpretation. Whereas papyri are largely the domain of
elite males, inscriptions provide much more social-history information
from all classes, men and women alike, because they include tomb-
stones, lists of names, curses, love messages, advertisements, and other
forms of everyday information.

Having considered the literary sources, we will explore the embar-
rassment of riches in the epigraphic evidence, looking for inscribed
words from Ephesus and beyond that mention Artemis of the Ephesians or those associated with her cult at the time of the earliest Christians. The sheer quantity of data necessitates summarizing.

ARTEMIS OF THE EPHESIANS BEYOND EPHESUS

As described in Pausanias's writings, references to Artemis of Ephesus
in stone are spread over a wide geographic area. The online concor-
dance identifies inscriptions mentioning her as far from Ephesus as
Attica; the Peloponnese; central Greece; northern Greece; the Aegean
islands, including Crete; Egypt; Nubia; and Cyrenaïca.[4]

---

[3]Horsley, "Inscriptions," 167.
[4]Since the time of this online search, a two-volume set that includes English translation of some inscriptions has come into print: Przemysław Siekierka, Krystyna Stebnicka and Aleksander Wolicki,
Women and the Polis: Public Honorific Inscriptions for Women in the Greek Cities from the Late Classical to

These, added to inscriptions from towns as close as eight miles from Ephesus's ruins, provide a wealth of information relevant to the city from outside its boundaries. In these writings "we have a major lexical resource for comparative study with the NT, localized to one area even if not exactly specific to the city itself in every case."[5] Their existence "holds out an excellent opportunity to assess how Greek was employed in certain linguistic registers and epigraphic genres."[6] Happily, the use of inscriptions in scholarship is slowly gaining momentum.

The database of inscriptions from Ephesus and surrounding towns reveals that many stones bear patrons' names, dedicatory plaques, funerary information, and lists of trade-guild members. Although some inscriptions are broken and many have yet to be recorded, plenty of evidence exists far beyond Ephesus itself to demonstrate that the epigraphic evidence complements the literary sources' emphases on Artemis's role as the city's preeminent deity and her ability to protect.

ARTEMIS IN EPHESUS

A quick search done a few years ago of Greek gods' names found in the epigraphic evidence in the ruins of Ephesus revealed the preeminence of the Ephesian Artemis:

- Artemis, 356 in Greek; 23 in Latin
- Isis, 4
- Dionysus, 1
- Zeus, 1
- Apollo, 1
- Athena, 0

---

the *Roman Period*, 2 vols. (Berlin: De Gruyter, 2021). I have included a few selections from Ephesus. The entries are from the vol. 2 section on Ephesus. Also, as a reminder, Nubia is south of Khartoum in Sudan and Cyrenaïca includes the eastern part of Libya.

[5]Horsley, "Inscriptions," 159.

[6]Horsley, "Inscriptions," 160.

A broader search today would need to include different forms of the
names (for example, "Artemis," "Artemidos," "Diana," "Artemis of the
Ephesians"). But the original gives a sense of the goddess's preeminence.
Some inscriptions refer to *the goddess* without identifying her, and the
chances are good that they refer to Artemis, but because one does not
always know for certain, we will limit ourselves to proper names unless
contextual clues confirm her identity.

Numerous inscriptions proclaim Artemis's greatness. A sampling
of the range of what archaeologists have found includes a praise
hymn offered to her,[7] mentions of annual sacrifices to her,[8] descriptions of the renown of the temple,[9] prayers and thanksgiving
offered to her,[10] attestation to her connection with the city,[11]
mention of virgins bringing decorations to her,[12] her great reputation outside of Ephesus,[13] and sacrifices given to her in homage.[14]
There is even a curse invoking Artemis's rage against anyone uri-
nating near the inscription.[15]

The epigraphic evidence also contains an abundance of Artemis
theophorics—that is, human names derived from Artemis and given to
both men and women. One moniker matches a name in the New Testament: *Artemas*, meaning "gift of Artemis." Paul wrote that he was
thinking of sending a man with this name to Titus (Titus 3:12).

Other names derived from Artemis include "Artemeis, Artemidora,
Artemisia, Artemon, Artemoneikes, Artemonis, and Artemidoros—a
particularly frequent name with about 100 people attested."[16] Some
names appear with relative frequency, others only once.

---

[7]SGI, Eph 829.
[8]SGI, Eph 212.
[9]SGI, Eph 115.
[10]SGI, Eph 1068; IEph 960, col. 2; IEph 967.
[11]SGI, Eph 3595.
[12]JOAI 55.
[13]SGI, Eph 163.
[14]SGI, Eph 228.
[15]SGI, Eph 2872.
[16]Horsley, "Inscriptions," 142.

While the task of sorting through human names might seem irrelevant, the range of theophorics in Ephesus derived from Artemis's name "cannot be merely coincidental, given that etymology was indubitably more significant in antiquity than is usual today in European societies."[17] The abundance of Artem- names suggests widespread parental devotion to the goddess expressed in their choices of names for their children.[18]

Artemis is frequently listed as the honoree of a building or statue dedication[19] in monuments erected by couples or families,[20] individuals,[21] and guilds.[22] Her priestesses are also honored with monuments.[23] Artemis is associated with the city's festivals, parades, athletics, and public honors.

Female officeholders in her cult, rather than coming to their positions with the expectation of payment for services rendered, financed works themselves and served as generous benefactors, which brought themselves and their families public honor. This financial detail suggests a degree of autonomy for women holding positions in service to Artemis.

Taken as a whole, the inscriptions provide many details that help historians form a picture of women's influence in Ephesus. The epigraphic record also complements the literary record in providing evidence that the goddess is seen as having power to bring women safely through that most feared of passages, childbirth. Such saving might mean the safe delivery of a child, but it might also mean a mercy killing with swift, painless death arrows. In this way the goddess might spare a woman from languishing for days before expiring. The epigraphic sources that describe Artemis hint at these qualities in addition to her volatility.

---

[17]Horsley, "Inscriptions," 142.
[18]Horsley, "Inscriptions," 142.
[19]IEph 1519.f.I; IEph 1908; IEph 2037; IEph 1914.2.
[20]IEph 438; IEph 411; IEph 429; IEph 424.
[21]IEph 857; IEph 829.
[22]IEph 1503.
[23]IEph 980, IEph 1710.

Of particular interest are the titles directly attributed to Artemis. I have found thirty-one inscriptions in Ephesus alone mentioning or dedicated to Artemis as "lord" (*kyria*). Oster provides a summary of her titles: "She was acclaimed as Artemis of the first throne (πρωτοθρόνιος), the Queen of the Cosmos (Βασιλῄς κόσμου), Lord (Κυρία), Savior (Σώτειρα) and a heavenly goddess (οὐράνιος θεὸς Ἄρτεμις Ἐφεσία) whose very nature and character could only be described in superlatives."[24] These superlatives he adds include "most high/greatest/highest/maximum" (μεγίστη); "most holy" (ἁγιωτάτη); and "splendid/glorious/ remarkable" (ἐπιφανεστάτη).[25]

THE CULT OF ARTEMIS IN THE INSCRIPTIONS

In addition to seeing how inscriptions describe Artemis herself, a look at participation in her cult, especially participation by women, provides further insight. Baugh's definitions of some religious job titles along with their meanings aid in understanding:

- **Priestess**: One who performed cultic duties in processions; provided financial underwriting of the cult. Some were young girls.

- *Kosmeteira*: Responsible for adornment of the cult statue of Artemis for a festival; often also the priestess of Artemis.

- *Prytanis*: Person who held the priesthood of Hestia Boulaia in the Prytaneion (seat of government); financial underwriting of the cult.

- *High priestess of Asia*: Responsible for the financial upkeep of the imperial cult. Cultic duties probably focused on divinized empresses; two are known to exist in Ephesus from the late first century.[26]

---

[24]Oster, "Religious Center," 1724; citing inscriptions FiE 2, no. 27.112; 20.6, 20.

[25]Oster, "Religious Center," 1724.

[26]S. M. Baugh, "A Foreign World: Ephesus in the First Century," in *Women in the Church: An Analysis and Application of 1 Timothy 2:9-15*, 2nd ed., ed. Andreas J. Köstenberger and Thomas R. Schreiner (Grand Rapids, MI: Baker Academic, 2005), 28.

- *Gymnasiarc*: Oversaw culture and education in gymnasia; financial underwriting.[27]

Below is a sampling of some of the more significant inscriptions in which one sees these titles.

Dated 27 BCE/ca. 88 CE. An honorary inscription from the Byzantine baths mentions a priestess of Artemis:

> The council and the people honored Vipsania Olympias, daughter of Lusius Vipsanius Appelles son of Neon, of the Cornelia tribe, and of Claudia Polemonis, daughter of Pythes. She held the priesthood of Artemis as befits the holy office, fulfilling both mysteries and sacrifices worthily; she crowned the temple and all its precincts on the splendid days consecrated to the goddess, organized public sacrifices, made distributions to the council and the gerousia [elders], [and] added five thousand denarii for repair of the basilica. She was the priestess in the prytany of Gaius Licinnius Dionysadoros.[28]

Note the presence of female priests. Observe also that this priesthood could be held by another simultaneously. Also, the familial relationship described here is that of daughters to parents rather than wives to husbands. Note too the mention of cult characteristics, such as mysteries and sacrifices. The person in the position of priestess "made distributions," which involved benevolence. This detail suggests office-holders were members of the upper class. Perhaps the daughters are virgin girls spending their parents' money in the role of benefactor, but nothing in the inscription other than the priestess's unmarried status suggests such to be the case.

A shrine dedicated to a woman named Pomponia Faustina also identifies the honoree as "priestess of Artemis," which appears to have been a hereditary office. Both her office and her husband—an unusual detail—are mentioned. While priestesses of Artemis were said to be

---

[27]Baugh, "A Foreign World," 18.
[28]*IvE* 987, 988; Siekierka, Stebnicka, and Wolicki, *Women*, 2:733-86.

virgins who dedicated their lives to the goddess, perhaps Pomponia Faustina married after she served as priestess of Artemis and was remembered later for her service.[29]

Dated second century CE. Few literary pieces—such as oracles, poems, and speeches—appear in the inscriptions. But in rare instances where they do, such as in this oracle attributed to Apollo, one finds a wealth of information:

> [For help, you have to look to] Artemis with the golden quiver, born from my family; for she is the ancestral leader of the entire town from its origin, midwife and augmenter of mortals, giver of harvest. Her form bring in from Ephesus, brilliant with gold. Put her up in a temple, full of joy: she will provide deliverance from your affliction and will dissolve the poison (or: magic) of pestilence, which destroys men, and will melt down with her flame-bearing torches in nightly fire the kneaded works of wax, the signs of the evil art of a sorcerer. But when you have performed for the goddess my decrees, worship with hymns the shooter of arrows, the irresistible, straight shooting one, and with sacrifices, her, the renowned and vigilant virgin; and during dancing and feasting, you girls together with the boys, above the salty lands of Maeonic Hermus, praising her in every respect wear crowns of large myrtle, having called from the Ephesian Land the pure Artemis, in order that she might always be to you an unfailing helper. If you should not fulfill the rites, then you will pay the penalty of fire.
>
> An oracle given by Apollon.[30]

Details seen in the literary works about Artemis include: bearing a golden quiver; relative of Apollo; midwife; proximity to Ephesus; deliverer in affliction; arrow-bearing hunter; one who delivers; one who throws flame-bearing torches; straight shooter of arrows; one

---

[29]Ruth Marie Léger, "Artemis and Her Cult" (PhD diss., University of Birmingham, 2015), 126.

[30]Fritz Graf, "An Oracle Against Pestilence from a Western Anatolian Town," *Zeitschrift für Papyrologie und Epigraphik* 92 (1992): 269; IEph 27.

crowned with myrtle; an unfailing helper; and a vigilant virgin capable of delivering a penalty of fire. Mention of magic, sorcery, and pestilence are interesting additions, along with boy-girl dancing groups of worshipers wearing crowns of myrtle. These details, which date long after the primary literary sources and describe Artemis similarly, show the endurance of many characteristics. Of particular interest is her enduring role as midwife and description as one who delivers.

Dated 88–132 CE. An honorary inscription for husband and wife reads as follows:

> Husband: [—][31] of Artemis, benefactor of the people on account of his own every virtue and piety toward Artemis, and depth and trustworthiness of his science and on account of his devotion toward the people.

> Wife: (NN honored) Ammion daughter of Perigenes, wife of Herakleides Didymos son of Menis, on account of her own modesty and the devotion of her husband Herakleides toward the people.[32]

Note the mention here of a male follower of Artemis. The goddess is neither worshiped exclusively by women nor, apparently, perceived as anti-male. Modesty, as mentioned here and in New Testament contexts, had a strong class element—often suggesting the presence but not the flaunting of resources.

Dated 132/200 CE. An honorary inscription to a priestess of Artemis found in the Varius bath in Ephesus says,

> The council and the people of the first and greatest metropolis of Asia, twice *neokoros* of the Augusti, of the city of the Ephesians, honored Quintilia Varilla, priestess of Artemis, mother of many senators, daughter of Publius Quintilius Valens Varius, who built this work at his own cost for the fatherland.[33]

---

[31] The notation [—] in epigraphy indicates an abbreviated word that cannot be completed. See "Epigraphic conventions," https://latininscriptions.ashmus.ox.ac.uk/documents/EpigraphicConventions.pdf.

[32] IEph 683a; SEG 13.500; adapted from Siekierka, Stebnicka, and Wolicki, *Women*, 736.

[33] IEph 986; SEG 28.861; Siekierka, Stebnicka, and Wolicki, *Women*, 738.

References to Ephesus as the first and greatest metropolis of Asia abound.[34] Immendörfer observes that in the decades that followed Ephesus being named as the capital of Asia, the city "became the economic, governmental and cultural centre of the province." He cites "the first and greatest metropolis of Asia" as a description that "Ephesus carried proudly," noting it "appears in numerous inscriptions."[35]

The word *neokoros*, seen here and meaning "temple guardian," appears in Acts 19:35 in reference to the city's stewardship of Artemis's temple. In that passage the city clerk describes Ephesus as "the *keeper* of the temple of the great Artemis." In using the title *neokoros*, Oster says, "The city was affirming its divine appointment as the keeper and protector of the religion and cult of the goddess" and also "the recipient of the privileges and blessing which go with that office."[36] The city's preeminence as a temple guardian extended beyond keeping the Artemision (that is, the temple), as "twice *neokoros*" suggests. Ephesus is often described in inscriptions and coins as "twice *neokoros*," because in addition to the Artemis cult, the cult of the Sebastoi was dedicated in 89/90 to the Flavian imperial family.[37]

Notice that the honoree in the inscription, Quintilia Varilla, is mentioned without reference to a husband—though she is a mother of great men. The male connection is to her father, whom other inscriptions identify as a secretary of the council.[38] Quintilia Varilla also built public baths and latrines, which—combined with mention of senators—suggests noble status.

---

[34]Compare with IEph 4336.

[35]Michael Immendörfer, *Ephesians and Artemis: The Cult of the Great Goddess of Ephesus as the Epistle's Context*, Wissenschaftliche Untersuchungen zum Neuen Testament II, Reihe 436 (Tübingen: Mohr Siebeck, 2017), 93; IEph 467.

[36]Oster, "Religious," 1702.

[37]Attempts were made to establish the temple of the Sebasteion at Ephesus under Domitian (89–90 CE). See Steven J. Friesen, *Imperial Cults and the Apocalypse of John: Reading Revelation in the Ruins* (Oxford: Oxford Academic, 2001), 39-55.

[38]IEph 712b.

An inscription dated to the second century CE provides insight into a detail found in the book of Ephesians. The inscription says: "[—] for Flavia Papiane, wife of P(ublius) Vedius Antonius, father of the most eminent Antoninus, who had the Ephesian goddess as his heir."[39] Instead of gaining an inheritance from the goddess, as one might expect, Antoninus names the goddess as his heir. A human offering his inheritance to a god is the opposite of what one finds in the Psalms and the book of Ephesians. The psalmist prays, "YHWH is the portion of my inheritance and my cup . . . indeed, my inheritance is beautiful to me" (Ps 16:5, author's translation). In Paul's epistle to the Ephesians, perhaps alluding to this psalm, he describes his recipients as having experienced "adoption as his legal heirs" (Eph 1:5), who have received in the Holy Spirit "the down payment of our inheritance" (Eph 1:14). The connection of Artemis with inheritance was perhaps on Paul's mind as he sought to show Jesus Christ as superior to Artemis in writing to recipients living in a city dominated by her. While Artemis's followers bring her their inheritance, followers of Christ receive an inheritance from God, and that inheritance from God, which is neither gold nor silver, is God himself.

An honorary inscription dating to the second century CE found near the Artemision praises a woman for having held the priesthood of the goddess "in a holy and generous manner in the year when Attalis, the priestess of the goddess, was the *prytanis*." Another dating to the same time lists a woman named Pi(naria?) Paula Aratiane and describes her as the priestess of Artemis and the noble *theoros* (sacred ambassador) at the Great Olympia.[40] In a third one dating to the second century, a group of teachers joined to honor "Pontia Apelliane, who was a *lampadarchissa* of the goddess under the archonship of Hermippos and Elpidephoros."[41] The latter reveals one way

---

[39]IEph 3077; Siekierka, Stebnicka, and Wolicki, *Women*, 600, 739, 742.

[40]IEph 992A, IEph 894; Siekierka, Stebnicka, and Wolicki, *Women*, 743

[41]IEph 3068; adapted from Siekierka, Stebnicka, and Wolicki, *Women*, 744.

Artemis was celebrated—by an annual torch race in her honor, over which a female presided.[42]

Dated 132/ca. 260 CE. "[NN honored—daughter of the *prytanis*] and *gymnasiarch* and of the priestess and *kosmeteira* of Artemis and high priestess of the temples of Asia in Ephesus, mother of Aelia Prokla, the *kosmeteira* of Artemis. [NN] set up (the statue)."[43]

Twice the word *kosmeteira* appears in this inscription, identifying an unnamed mother responsible for festival adornment of the cult statue of Artemis and a high priestess of temples (plural) whose daughter is also a *kosmeteira* of Artemis. Adorning the goddess with apparel is such an important task in the Artemis cult that an office is needed to fulfill the role.

Dated 132/214 CE. Honorary inscription for Larcia Theognis Iuliane, *prytanis* and priestess of Artemis:

> The council and the people of the first and greatest metropolis of Asia, twice *neokoros* of the Augusti, the city of the Ephesians, honoured Larcia Theogenis Iuliana, the *prytanis* and *gymnasiarch* of all the gymnasia, the priestess of Lord Artemis, daughter of Aulus Larcius Hieron Iulianus, *prytanis* and *gymnasiarch* of all the gymnasia and sacred herald [—].[44]

Longfellow, in her work on epigraphic evidence, writes that the positions held by the *prytanis* and *archiereia*, or high priestess, were renewed annually. The women in these positions might hold them over the course of multiple years, so the inscriptions provide an overview of the officeholders' public life. Longfellow puts forth evidence that at least thirty females served as *prytanis*, which she describes as "the eponymous office holder for Ephesos, during the first through third centuries,"[45] making it "one of the two more common offices held by women in the

---

[42]IEph 814.
[43]IEph 994; author's adaptation from Siekierka, Stebnicka, and Wolicki, *Women*, 747.
[44]IEph 985; Siekierka, Stebnicka, and Wolicki, *Women*, 749.
[45]By the third century, the Artemision was in disrepair and the world of Ephesus differed significantly from that of the first and second centuries. Nevertheless, the number serves as a helpful estimate.

provincial capital."[46] The other common office, she says, "was the priesthood of Artemis." She explains that the office held by the *prytanis* required carrying out religious duties throughout the year, including participation in and funding of civic sacrifices and banquets connected with religious events.[47] Such funding once again reveals a connection between religious office and wealth in Ephesus.

Dated CE 180/192.

> To Good Fortune. For Claudia Kratia Veriana, of senatorial order, the *prytanis* and *gymnasiarch* of all the gymnasia, [---] with dignity [---], the priestess and *kosmeteira* of the most holy Artemis, who held the priesthood in a worthy manner and with dignity, daughter from the father's side of Claudius Metrobios Verianus son of [Claudius Me]trobios and Claudia Kratia, the high priests, and from the mother's side of Ulpia Demokratia, the *kosmeteira*, granddaughter of Iulia Damiana Polla, the *kosmeteira* and *prytanis*, great-granddaughter of Flavia Polla, the priestess and *kosmeteira*, great-great-granddaughter of Iulia Polla, the priestess, *kosmeteira*, high priestess and *prytanis*, and of Mindia Potentilla, the high priestess and *kosmeteira*. She (Claudia Kratia) is descended from the priestesses and *kosmeteirai*.[48]

Notice how the honoree of this *prytanis* and priestess of Artemis, Claudia Kratia, has a genealogy described in terms of the females.

---

[46]Brenda Longfellow, *Roman Imperialism and Civic Patronage: Form, Meaning, and Ideology in Monumental Fountain Complexes* (Cambridge: Cambridge University Press, 2014), 80.

[47]Longfellow, *Roman Imperialism*, 80.

[48]Longfellow, *Roman Imperialism*, 656-57. Siekierka, Stebnicka, and Wolicki observe, "More than 200 women known from the honorific inscriptions of the Roman period were priestesses of local cults and these cults were often specified. . . . In the imperial period, priesthoods, which were preserved for wealthy women from elite families, also served as the arena for public activity for women. In comparison with earlier periods . . . fewer women were publicly honoured for holding priestly office and the priestesses were praised not only for their *eusebeia* [piousness, reverence, duty fulfillment to gods], but also their *philotimia*, i.e., generosity during their term, especially for the expenses which exceeded the ordinary costs of holding priesthoods. . . . The priestesses of Artemis at Ephesos, the sisters Vipsaniae Polla and Olympias 'crowned the temple and all its precincts on the splendid days consecrated to the goddess, organized public sacrifices, made distributions to the council and the Gerousia, added five thousand denarii for repairs of the basilica'; Tryphosa, also the priestesses of Artemis, 'held the gymnasiarchy and donated 150 thousand denarii" (*Women*, 117).

While a father is mentioned in reference to rank, female relatives dominate the rest of the inscription. Other sources corroborate the mention of nobility: Iulia Polla, mentioned in the inscription, was the sister of the consul in 105 CE.[49] So, one sees both an upper-class connection with religious office and a connection to civic power.

An honorary inscription for a priestess of Artemis describes her carrying out her office in a "pious and orderly manner." She is described as having "renewed all the mysteries of the goddess and organized (them) according to the ancient custom."[50] The content of the mysteries is unknown, but it is worth noting that the apostle Paul in his epistle to the church in this same city references the mystery of the unity between heaven and earth in Christ (Eph 1:9-10).

Another inscription, which dates to the mid- to late second century, honors a woman named "[I]ulia Panteime Potentilla," who held the office of priestess of Artemis. This priestess is "probably the same person as the well-known benefactress of Ephesos Iulia Potentilla."[51] If so, this inscription once again supports the hypothesis that females associated with Artemis and her cult were from the homes of the wealthy. Notice also the wealth implied in this honorary inscription dating to the first century CE:

[The council and the people honoured Claudia Caninia Severa], *femina clarissima* of consular ancestors, the priestess and *kosmeteira* of the [Lord] Artemis, pious *prytanis*, *theros* at the Great Olympia, daughter of Tiberius Claudius Severus, the first consul from Ephesos, and Caninia Gargonilla of consular ancestors. She embellished our fatherland with many great works.[52]

Dated to the first or second century CE, the honorary inscription below is dedicated to a female named Tryphosa, whose name matches

[49]IEph 980; Siekierka, Stebnicka, and Wolicki, *Women*, 757.
[50]IEph 3059; Siekierka, Stebnicka, and Wolicki, *Women*, 761.
[51]IEph 983; Siekierka, Stebnicka, and Wolicki, *Women*, 762.
[52]IEph 892; Siekierka, Stebnicka, and Wolicki, *Women*, 765.

that of a woman whom Paul describes in Romans 16:12 as a "[laborer]
in the Lord."

> When T(itus) Fla(vius) Arist[—] was the priest, the village of the Bo-
> nitai honored Tryphosa, daughter of Artemas son of Ephagathos son
> of Ephagathos, son of Dionysios and the mother of Diadoumenis. She
> was the priestess of Artemis, held the *gymnasiarchy* and donated
> 150 thousand denarii.[53]

The Tryphosa in this inscription has a father, Artemas, the same name
Paul mentions in his letter to Titus (3:12). This is not to say that the
Tryphosa or Artemas found in inscriptions were the same people men-
tioned in the New Testament, but these names have implications for
how scholars understand the social status of the members of the
Pauline churches.

Below is a sampling of phrases culled from Baugh's work, which includes another full page of inscriptions naming women with some relationship to the Artemis cult. Notice the offices they held:

- "mo[ther] (?)Chaeremon, Kallinoe who was appointed Priestess
  of Artemis by the People of the Ephesians"[54]

- "daughter of Publius, Priestess (of Artemis) and High Priestess
  of Asia"[55]

- "Ulpia Junilla, Priestess, daughter of the Incredible Ulpius Tro-
  phimus and of U[lpia?] Agathemeris, completed her term as
  Priestess with piety and decorum. In the *prytany* of Julia Polla"[56]

- "The daughter of Flavia Meltine . . . [made] all the distributions of
  her priesthood and gave to the city 5,000 denarii, they (Flavia
  Meltine her mother, daughter of Maior, and Maior her grandfather,

---

[53]IEph 3239 A; SEG 31.959; Siekierka, Stebnicka, and Wolicki, *Women*, 735.

[54]S. M. Baugh, "Cult Prostitution in New Testament Ephesus: A Reappraisal," *Journal of the Evangelical Theological Society* 42, no. 3 (September 1999): 453. *IvE* 615A; dated to late 1 BCE?

[55]Baugh, "Cult Prostitution," 454; *IvE* 1017, dated to 93–100 CE.

[56]Baugh, "Cult Prostitution," 454; *IvE* 989A.

and Maior the Younger her uncle) gave it to the city from their own funds"[57]

- "Julia Pantima Potentilla, Priestess and *Kosmeteira* of Artemis, daughter of Julius Artemas"[58]

- "The State Council and People honor Mindia Menandra, daughter of Gaius Mindius Amoenus, who completed her term as Priestess of the goddess purely and generously"[59]

- "[Aurelia ? Priestess of Arte]mis, completed her term of Priestess piously and with decorum, restored all the rites of the goddess and funded (them) in accord with ancient custom, daughter of M. Aur(elius) Hierokleos Apolinarius the emperor-honoring General, Market-Director, Council Chairman, father of the Priestess"[60]

Rogers observes that the list of offices held includes several women who attended Olympic games as official representatives. Women's presence as representatives of the city "symbolizes the possibilities open to at least some women at the beginning of the second century A.D."[61]

In conclusion, what does the epigraphic evidence reveal about people associated with the Artemis cult? Interestingly, the inscriptions are silent on these points:

- *They provide no evidence of cult prostitution.* In addition to the literary sources, the inscriptions contain no hint of such prostitution in Ephesus. If anything, the opposite appears to be the case: virginity and celibacy dominate.

- *They reveal nothing suggesting an anti-male nor a woman-power mentality.* The inscriptions do have a strong female emphasis. Those

---

[57]Baugh, "Cult Prostitution," 454; *IvE* 997.

[58]Baugh, "Cult Prostitution," 455, *IvE* 983, dated to 177–180 CE.

[59]Baugh, "Cult Prostitution," 454; *IvE* 992; side A.

[60]Baugh, "Cult Prostitution," 454-55; *IvE* 3059, second to third century.

[61]Guy MacLean Rogers, "The Constructions of Women at Ephesos," *Zeitschrift für Papyrologie und Epigraphik* 90 (1992): 223.

that mention mothers and grandmothers—perhaps because the offices were inherited from them—tend to omit the names of male family members. Nevertheless, nothing in them suggests that a feminine principle is prevalent in Ephesus nor does anything hint at attempts at switching gender roles or suggest hostility between male and female.

- *They do not suggest that Artemis was a sex or fertility goddess.* People holding offices within her cult appear to have been, like her, almost exclusively virginal.[62] Again, Artemis is nobody's mother.

Descriptions of Artemis's cult and those associated with it include an emphasis on wealth and honor, with women officeholders coming from the upper classes and appearing to have some autonomy in their benevolence. These women held a variety of honorable titles, such as *priestess*, *prytanis*, *lampadarchissa*, *kosmeteira*, and *gymnasiarch*. Those honored are most often mentioned apart from male authority, probably unmarried, and described as making distributions, dedicating altars and statues, and financing inscriptions.

---

[62]See Sandra L. Glahn, "The Identity of Artemis in First-Century Ephesus," *Bibliotheca Sacra* 172 (July–Sept 2015): 316-34.

5

ARTEMIS IN ARCHITECTURE AND ART

ALTHOUGH EPHESUS WAS ONCE a renowned seaport with multiple harbors, today it is silted in, and its closest port is Kuşadasi, ten miles southwest of the historic site. The metropolis exists only in ruins, though *ruins* hardly seems to be an appropriate descriptor, as the site is spectacular (as far as abandoned cities go).[1] At one time Ephesus stood at the crossroads of six cultures and attracted such notable people as Paul, Luke, Timothy, John, Priscilla, Aquila, and Apollos, not to mention King Croesus, Alexander the Great, Antony, and Cleopatra.

By the late 1980s, only about 20 percent of the city's ruins had been excavated after more than a century of work. That percentage has remained constant for the past four decades.[2] Yet even in that mere 20 percent, one still finds the streets of Ephesus lined with pillars. Statues and mosaic sidewalks hint of its former opulence. Colored tiles in geometric patterns outline perimeters where shops, restaurants, gambling houses, public buildings, a brothel, and aristocrats' trendy homes once served about two hundred thousand inhabitants during the Roman period.[3]

---

[1]Bunny McBride, "Ephesus," *Christian Science Monitor*, May 7, 1986, www.csmonitor.com/1986/0507/zephe-f.html.
[2]McBride, "Ephesus."
[3]Michael Immendörfer, *Ephesians and Artemis: The Cult of the Great Goddess of Ephesus as the Epistle's Context*, Wissenschaftliche Untersuchungen zum Neuen Testament II, Reihe 436 (Tübingen: Mohr Siebeck, 2017), 93.

In 1863, British engineer John Turtle Wood excavated Ephesus's ruins on behalf of the British Museum. By the end of the century, Austrian archaeologists had taken over and partnered with Turkish archaeologists. In 2015, UNESCO added Ephesus to their World Heritage List, and today it receives about two million visitors per year, making it one of the most visited sites in the world. Its art and architecture continue to provide new clues about the nature of the Artemis cult there at the time of the earliest Christians.

THE ARTEMISION

Artemis's temple, the Artemision, once stood adjacent to the city, crowning the main harbor. The first such temple dedicated to Artemis dates to 550 BCE. That version burned down in 356 BCE, leaving people to speculate as to how such a thing could happen. As the literary sources revealed, Plutarch quotes someone who posited that Artemis could not protect her temple because she was away fulfilling midwifery duties as she officiated the birth of Alexander the Great.[4]

In its prime, the Artemision towered at four times the size of the Parthenon on Athens's acropolis. Outlined by 127 Ionic columns that stood 60 feet high, the Artemision was 450 feet long and 228 feet wide. Here's how Pliny the Elder described it in 77 CE:

> The most wonderful monument of Græcian magnificence, and one that merits our genuine admiration, is the Temple of Diana at Ephesus, which took one hundred and twenty years in building, a work in which all Asia joined. . . . The entire length of the temple is four hundred and twenty-five feet, and the breadth, two hundred and twenty-five. The columns are one hundred and twenty-seven in number, and sixty feet high, each presented by a different king. Thirty-six of these columns are carved, and one by the hand of Scopas.[5]

---

[4]Plutarch, *Life of Alexander* 3.3, was mentioned in the chapter on literary sources.
[5]Pliny the Elder, *The Natural History*, trans. John Bostock and H. T. Riley (London: Taylor and Francis, 1855), 36.21. www.perseus.tufts.edu/hopper/text?doc=Perseus%3Atext%3A1999.02.0137%3Abook%3D 36%3Achapter%3D21#note3.

After Goths destroyed the Artemision in 263 CE, the building remained in use through the fourth century, though it was only partially
rebuilt. In late antiquity, builders scavenged its stones for building materials. Eight of its columns, green marble beauties, still support the
Hagia Sofia in Istanbul. Because the temple was built on marshy ground
to preserve it through earthquakes, it disappeared by degrees—sinking,
crumbling, and being pilfered a few stones at a time.[6] Only a lone pillar,
cobbled together from fallen stone, marks the spot where the temple
once stood. Storks, longtime inhabitants at the site, crown the pillar's
capital with their nest.

Inside the rebuilt temple, according to Pliny the Elder, stood statues—
representations of Amazons.[7] Literary and epigraphic sources mention
statues of Artemis made of bronze or wood decorated with gold. Coins
also bear the goddess's images.[8] Pausanias labels one of these statues as
"Artemis Savior."[9] He also references statues, images, and shrines of Artemis Ephesia seen outside of Ephesus. Today one such statue is in Jordan,
more than 1,000 miles away—evidencing the cult's renown.

According to Muss, when John Chrysostom stayed in Ephesus
(401 CE), he prohibited continuing the practice of Artemis worship in
the Artemision by stripping the cult statue of Artemis down to its

---

[6]Ruth Marie Léger, "Artemis and Her Cult" (PhD diss., University of Birmingham, 2015), 111.

[7]Pliny the Elder (23/24–79 CE) records that five bronze statues of Amazons stood in the Artemision
of Ephesus (*Natural History* 34.19). He cites a fifth-century-BCE artist competition to account for this
quantity of sculptures bearing the same theme concentrated in one location: "The most celebrated of
these artists, though born at different epochs, have joined in a trial of skill in the Amazons which
they have respectively made. When these statues were dedicated in the Temple of Diana [Artemis] at
Ephesus, it was agreed, in order to ascertain which was the best, that it should be left to the judgment
of the artists themselves who were then present: upon which, it was evident that that was the best,
which all the artists agreed in considering as the next best to his own. Accordingly, the first rank was
assigned to Polycletus, the second to Phidias, the third to Cresilas, the fourth to Cydon, and the fifth
to Phradmon."

[8]For gold, see Pliny, *Natural History* 16.79. Regarding coins: "[Artemis Ephesia] appears on many coins,
not only of the Ephesian mint but of other cities which wished to honour the goddess. Indeed, it is
probably safe to say that no other famous ancient statue was so frequently depicted in coins." Charles
Seltman, "The Wardrobe of Artemis," *The Numismatic Chronicle and Journal of the Royal Numismatic
Society (Sixth Series)* 12, no. 42 (1952): 34.

[9]Pausanias, *Description of Greece*, trans. W. H. S. Jones, Loeb Classical Library (Cambridge, MA: Harvard
University Press, 1918), 1.37.1-1.41.2.

archaic wooden cult image, the *xoanon*, robbing it of jewelry and allowing it to be burned.[10] In the temple's place, The Church of the Virgin Mary was dedicated to the *Theotokos*, the "Mother of God," a name confirmed at the Council of Ephesus in 431. This dedication consecrated a place which for centuries "had represented the most perfect expression of pagan religiosity."[11] The Virgin replaced the virgin.

About two miles from the ruins, the Ephesus Archaeological Museum displays two life-sized statues of Artemis dating to New Testament times. Curators consider these statues the museum's prime pieces, preeminent in the cache of artifacts collected since 1863.

The best-known Artemis iconography is that of the maiden who inspired contemporary Wonder Woman—beautiful and young, sometimes bearing a shield, often carrying a bow and a quiver full of arrows. She is sometimes flanked with dogs or deer (see fig. 5.1). A *chitōn*, the skirt-like or girded garment suitable for active pursuits, drapes her frame, though sometimes fabric covers her feet.

This representation of Artemis—the classic maiden image—appears in Ephesus. But so does the Artemis of the Ephesians image, which looks quite different (see fig. 5.2). The latter is known for its bulbous appendages on Artemis's chest. Inhabitants of the city seem to have interpreted them as two visions of the same person. The Artemis described as *Artemis of the Ephesians* is covered with images and ornamentation, much of which was "removable and renewable, according to ancient testimonia on

Figure 5.1. Diana of Versailles or Artemis, Goddess of the Hunt (AD 1st or 2nd century), The Louvre Museum. Photo by Sandra Glahn.

---

[10]Ulrike Muss, "The Artemision in Early Christian Times," *Early Christianity* 7 (2016): 293-312, 309.
[11]Muss, "The Artemision," 312.

festivals, cultic inscriptions from Ephesus, and literary anecdotes."[12] On coins, in paintings, and in statues, the exotic, cult Artemis has an altogether different look from the classic, hunting Artemis.

Some coins bear on one side a bust of the bow-and-arrow-bearing Artemis, and on the other, the version of Artemis with bulbous appendages. The goddess's two personas, while having the same story, have strikingly different visual features (compare figs. 5.1 and 5.2). The bow-bearing hunter version is self-explanatory based on the literary record describing her exploits. But the exotic version requires explanation.

Figure 5.2. Artemis of the Ephesians (ca. 4th century BC), Pio Clementino Museum, The Vatican. Photo by Joe Fantin.

THE *DIOPET* AND HEADGEAR

Artemis Ephesia sometimes wears a crown or headdress (fig. 5.2). Morris says, "A tall head-dress, especially when shaped into the walls of a city, crowned both prehistoric and early Greek goddesses." Having walls atop a goddess's head expresses in visible form "the protection a deity (often a goddess) affords her city." In effect, the goddess wears on her head what she protects.[13]

---

[12]Sarah P. Morris, "The Prehistoric Background of Artemis Ephesia: A Solution to the Enigma of Her 'Breasts'?," *Der Kosmos der Artemis von Ephesos. Sonderschriften des Österreichischen Archäologischen Instituts* 37 (2001): 38.

[13]Morris, "Prehistoric Background," 138-39. Also, LiDonnici writes, "Artemis Ephesia most often wears a simple *polos* and veil, a large basket (κάλαθος), or a replica of a shrine or temple. These temple crowns may have political resonance if . . . they refer to the *neocorate* temples of the emperor and Rome at Ephesus or to the city's wealth, kept in the treasuries of the Artemision. Fleischer believes (*Artemis von Ephesos*, 58) that the appearance of the mural crown on coins and on E 66, a statuette of the first century CE, indicate that a mural crown was an element of the central image's adornment through Trajanic and Hadrianic times. If this is so, its disappearance in the later Roman Empire may be a further reflection of the erosion of the political dimension of the Ephesians' understanding of their goddess and its corresponding universalization." Lynn R. LiDonnici, "The Images of Artemis Ephesia and Greco-Roman Worship: A Reconsideration." *Harvard Theological Review* 85, no. 4 (Oct 1992): 395.

A connection may exist between Artemis's headgear and the artifact described in the book of Acts as Zeus-fallen, or *diopetous* (διοπετοῦς, Acts 19:35). Arthur Cook, a British archaeologist and Zeus scholar, described an artifact found at Smyrna that came from Ephesus.[14] It was identified as a greenish sacred stone dated to 2000 BCE and similar to others thought to be endowed with life or to give access to a deity, most commonly Zeus.[15] He saw it as having a quasi-human shape. A tin band encircled it (see figs. 5.3 and 5.4), and from the band hung four pairs of tin pendants symmetrically placed. Finally, at the foot, opposite each pendant, was a hole for the insertion of a stud, perhaps of amber.[16] He considered the possibility that the piece was the Zeus-fallen image of Artemis Ephesia, noting, "And all the more so, when we learn that, by an impressive coincidence, the pounder actually came from Ephesos."[17]

Figures 5.3 and 5.4. *Diopet* (or "Zeus-fallen") of Ephesus (date unknown), National Museums Liverpool, World Museum, accession number 49.18.87. Photo by Barbara Rowan, 2022. Used with permission.

---

[14]Arthur B. Cook, *Zeus: A Study in Ancient Religion*, vol. 3 (Cambridge: Cambridge University Press, 1940), 898.

[15]K. P. Oakley, "The *Diopet* of Ephesus," *Folklore* 82, no. 3 (Autumn 1971): 207.

[16]Cook, *Zeus*, 899.

[17]Cook, *Zeus*, 900.

The piece was sold to the City of Liverpool Museums,[18] which identified it not as a meteorite, but as a terrestrial rock.[19] Whether or not the piece in the Liverpool Museums' possession is the *diopet* mentioned in Acts, it affords readers a look at the possibilities for what the city clerk of Ephesus could have meant in referencing a Zeus-fallen image. Additionally, the symmetrically placed pairs of tin pendants may provide clues as to the meaning of the bulbous items on the goddess's torso. It has been suggested the *diopet* would fit perfectly on the statue's crown.

THE TORSO

Moving from head to neckline on the Artemis Ephesia statue, one sees signs of the zodiac placed above rows of small, bulbous appendages worn like a necklace. Arnold interprets the zodiacal art as conveying that Artemis possesses "authority and power superior to that of astrological fate."[20]

Below the images of Gemini and Cancer on the statue's midriff, one sees the most identifiable feature of Artemis Ephesia statues: the bulbous-shaped appendages. Most who describe Artemis as a mother and fertility goddess point to these protuberances to support their theory. The logic goes something like this: Artemis is female and has many breasts; breasts are both sexual and designed for maternal nurturing; therefore, Artemis must be a nurturing mother and fertility goddess.

It has been argued here already that no evidence exists in the literary or epigraphic sources linking Artemis with sex, mothering, or reproduction/fertility. But if such is the case, why does a Google search of *Artemis + fertility goddess* generate more than three-quarters of a million hits? And why would an A&E documentary on the Seven

---

[18]Margaret Warhurst, "The Danson Bequest and Merseyside County Museums," *Archaeological Reports* 24 (1977–1978): 85-88.

[19]Oakley, "The *Diopet*," 207.

[20]Clinton E. Arnold, *Ephesians: Power and Magic: The Concept of Power in Ephesians in Light of Its Historical Setting* (Grand Rapids, MI: Baker Academic, 1992), 32.

Wonders of the Ancient World describe Artemis in Ephesus as part of "an ancient fertility cult"?[21] This depiction of her comes from a confluence of several sources: conflation of her persona through the centuries, Christian polemics, and incorrect interpretation.

Some see a connection to fertility because they see a conflation of Artemis with the Anatolian goddess who long preceded the Ephesian Artemis on the site. Their understanding of this Anatolian goddess influences people's connection with the later Artemis and mothering.[22] It is true that a Neolithic goddess linked to the site was eventually replaced by Artemis, but that does not mean that the goddess on the site in the fifth century BCE was the same as the one worshiped centuries later. Others merge Artemis with the mother god Kybele, but in doing so, Morris says, "we have neglected ancient distinction" between them.[23]

Others see breasts when they look at the statue and are influenced in their interpretation by Christian polemics. The earliest key sources describing Ephesians Artemis as multibreasted were third- and fourth-century CE authors Minucius Felix and Jerome.[24] The former wrote, "Diana sometimes is a hunter, with her robe girded up high; and as the Ephesian she has many and fruitful breasts (*mammis multis*)."[25] Jerome wrote in a letter to Paula and Eustochium, "The Ephesians honor Diana, not the famous hunter, but Diana of the many breasts whom the Greeks call *polymaston*, so as to make people believe by this image that she nourishes all animals and all living things."

Note that neither of the abovementioned writers recognizes the two manifestations of the goddess as the same person. LiDonnici observes that the date of Jerome's comment is "387 CE, after the Gothic

---

[21]*Ancient Mysteries: Seven Wonders of the Ancient World* (New York: A&E Video, 2005).

[22]Andrew E. Hill, "Ancient Art and Artemis: Explaining the Polymastic Nature of the Figurine," *Journal of Ancient Near Eastern Studies* 21 (1992): 91.

[23]Morris, "Prehistoric Background," 141.

[24]Minucius Felix, *The Octavius*, trans. Robert Ernest Wallis, 23.5, https://ccel.org/ccel/felix/octavius/anf04.iv.iii.xxi.html; Jerome, personal letter to Paula and Eustochium as part of Prologue to *Commentariorum in epistolam ad Ephesios proem* (PL 26.441).

[25]Minucius Felix, *Octavius* 23.5.

destruction of the Artemision in 265 CE," and she posits, "It is possible that after 265 people's ideas of Artemis Ephesia and Ephesian worship were based solely on the representations, rather than the actual central statue."[26] Trebilco and Oster—both eminent Ephesus scholars sympathetic to Christianity—conclude that the fertility-goddess view of the cult stems from the Christian polemic against Artemis.[27]

These factors have all contributed to the misidentification of the rounded objects on the Ephesian Artemis as breasts. But scholars find at least four problems with this view:

1. *They lack nipples and areolas.* For breasts to nurture, they must have nipples. The protuberances on Artemis's front lack a means by which to nurture.

2. *Males have them.* Male figures, such as Zeus, bear similar frontal imagery without having maternal properties. Rather than body parts, Fleischer sees the objects as a form of pectoral armor or breastplate.[28]

3. *The objects are not skin.* In fact, they differ in color from the statue's skin. Seeing them as something the goddess wears rather than as

---

[26]LiDonnici, "The Images," 392. Using past methodologies, historians might have simply accepted Jerome's statement about Artemis and her cult as the reality, but using new strategies of literary analysis, experts consider how much time, distance, and philosophical perspective stands between the person writing and the phenomena being described. Jerome was describing Artemis not as a former participant in her cult but as a Christian polemicist looking back on the first century from the fourth. As Baugh, writing on a different topic, observed, "Third-century Ephesus was quite different from Paul and Timothy's city." S. M. Baugh, "A Foreign World: Ephesus in the First Century," in *Women in the Church: An Analysis and Application of 1 Timothy 2:9-15,* 2nd ed., eds. Andreas J. Köstenberger and Thomas R. Schreiner (Grand Rapids, MI: Baker Academic, 2005), 14.

[27]Richard Oster, "The Ephesian Artemis 'Whom All Asia and the World Worship' (Acts 19:27): Representative Epigraphical Testimony to Ἄρτεμις Ἐφεσία outside Ephesos," in *Transmission and Reception: New Testament Text-Critical and Exegetical Studies,* ed. J. W. Childers and D. C. Parker (Piscataway, NJ: Gorgias Press, 2006), 24-44; Paul Trebilco, *The Early Christians in Ephesus from Paul to Ignatius* (Grand Rapids, MI: Eerdmans, 2007), 23. Also Morris: "[Artemis's] nurturing powers, whether promoted by Jerome's description of her as *nutrix* of all living creatures to her follows, or simply by her *uberrima* front, have inspired most visions of her both in art and in speculation. This image of her as an all-nurturing mother remains popular even in modern tourist art and souvenirs" ("Prehistoric Background," 41).

[28]R. Fleischer, *Artemis von Ephesus und Verwandte Kultstatuen aus Anatolien und Syrien,* EPRO 35 (Leiden: Brill, 1973), 79.

parts of her body helps account for why "they are not made of the same color as body parts on statues where face, hands, and feet are dark (in imitation of wood or ivory)" (see fig. 5.5).[29] The ebony face, hands, and feet set against white decorations make for a stark contrast.

4. *They are too low.* Placement of the rounded objects on the goddess's body is lower than where breasts belong (fig. 5.5). LiDonnici notes that they "are more rounded and can sit so low on the figure as to suggest more of a stomach ornament than a pectoral."[30]

So, what are they? One hypothesis is that Artemis's frontal features are bull scrota, but this is a late theory that some now label misogynistic, originating from people seeking to find in Artemis images of male power.[31] Others suggest Artemis's trunk-like legs, combined with the features on her chest, are designed to make her look like a date-palm tree, commemorating her birth in a grove. Some posit the frontal pieces are olives, which would

Figure 5.5. Artemis of Ephesus (2nd century), Naples Archaeological Museum. Photo by Gary Glahn.

---

[29]LiDonnici, "The Images," 141.

[30]LiDonnici, "The Images," 396.

[31]LiDonnici observes that "the theory's radical 'masculinization' of the symbols of Artemis Ephesia may reflect twentieth-century Western constructions of gender that tend to identify the categories 'power' and 'virility' with each other" ("The Images," 393). Morris says the bull-scrota view has been rejected by scholars due to the "lack of (male) cattle bones." She also notes that "specialists in Anatolian and Near Eastern cultures have recognized the chest decoration as a feature of prehistoric deities, schematic in early idols and executed in full in the first millennium" ("Prehistoric Background," 142).

connect the goddess with the olive grove mentioned by Strabo. Additional suggestions are eggs, deer canines, grapes, nuts, acorns, and inverted honeycombs—which would fit with the bee image on her side.

Do any of the theories have merit? Anton Bammer points the way. As mentioned, Austrians excavated in Ephesus for more than a century. Bammer, an Austrian architect and archaeologist, started digging as part of their team at age twenty-five. He spent the next fifty years as part of the Ephesus excavation team and has written several books on the findings. In an article for *Anatolian Studies*, Bammer describes how he discovered the ancient altar of Artemis's temple and some "holy garbage" from the original temple. There his team found more than five hundred gourd-shaped teardrop beads made of amber. They date back to 750–560 BCE. Most were pierced, and "all of the objects with holes must have been used to make large necklaces" which were linked to the frontal jewelry of the ancient *xoanon*—which is, as mentioned, the term for an early iteration of a cult's deity in ancient Greece.

The *xoanon* was probably the earliest idol worshiped at the site, and some researchers believe it was destroyed during an early flood that buried the perimeter of the temple.[32] Could the teardrop-shaped pieces of jewelry be later iterations of the tin teardrop-shaped pieces on the *diopet*, picking up the shape to repeat the motif?

The relationship between these pieces and the so-called eggs or breasts on Artemis's chest and around her neck, Bammer said, was evident. The pieces were jewelry, not body parts. Thus, in the mind of one of Ephesus's most credible archaeologists, a find at the excavation site during the 1987–1988 season fairly eliminated breasts as a credible option.

Five years after Bammer published his findings, he and his colleague, Ulrike Muss, directors of the Austrian excavations at the Artemision, marked the one hundredth year of Austrian excavations on the site

---

[32]A. Bammer, "A 'Peripteros' of the Geometric Period in the Artemision of Ephesus," *Anatolian Studies* 40 (1990): 137-209.

with a symposium. They invited archaeology scholar Sarah P. Morris to present her work on the prehistoric Artemis Ephesia, which she published in 2001.

Morris said that the amber shapes first found by Hogarth in 1908, along with the hundreds of pendants Bammer analyzed, were among the early jewelry associated with the goddess. These supported an "early date and home" for both the image of the goddess and the associated shapes.[33] Considering that Western Anatolia was once inhabited by Hittites, Morris saw a Hittite connection with the statue's imagery and proposed that the objects were comparable to Hittite pouches made of goatskin and sometimes decorated with stone beads, called *kurša*. These were known to be filled with magical material and used as fetishes. Often associated with protecting people and places, they were invoked in oaths and called on in magical rites.[34]

In both Greek and Anatolian myth and ritual, an animal skin "is the key to power and prosperity,"[35] Morris says. So she concludes, "If a *kurša* could be made or decorated with stone beads as well as leather animal-skins, then the amber beads found in the early levels of the Artemision are even closer to prehistoric Hittite cult attributes."[36]

If Bammer and Morris are correct, the visual record aligns with the literary and epigraphic sources that link Artemis with magic. The inscriptions include incantations. And in the literary record, the author of Acts tells a story about magicians in Ephesus right before his report of the disturbance in Ephesus about Artemis:

> God was performing extraordinary miracles by Paul's hands, so that when even handkerchiefs or aprons that had touched his body were brought to the sick, their diseases left them and the evil spirits went out

---

[33]Morris, "Prehistoric Background," 142.

[34]Morris, "Prehistoric Background," 135-51, 143. For a popular-level description of Morris's findings, see Marg Mowczko, "The Regalia of Artemis Ephesia," *Marg Mowczko*, July 23, 2016, https://margmowczko.com/regalia-artemis-ephesia/.

[35]Morris, "Prehistoric Background," 143.

[36]Morris, "Prehistoric Background," 144.

of them. But some itinerant Jewish exorcists tried to invoke the name
of the Lord Jesus over those who were possessed by evil spirits, saying,
"I sternly warn you by Jesus whom Paul preaches." (Now seven sons of a
man named Sceva, a Jewish high priest, were doing this.) But the evil
spirit replied to them, "I know about Jesus and I am acquainted with
Paul, but who are you?" Then the man who was possessed by the evil
spirit jumped on them and beat them all into submission. He prevailed
against them so that they fled from that house naked and wounded. This
became known to all who lived in Ephesus, both Jews and Greeks; fear
came over them all, and the name of the Lord Jesus was praised. Many
of those who had believed came forward, confessing and making their
deeds known. Large numbers of those who had practiced magic collected their books and burned them up in the presence of everyone.
When the value of the books was added up, it was found to total
50,000 silver coins. In this way the word of the Lord continued to grow
in power and to prevail. (Acts 19:11-20)

Of this episode, Arnold makes two key observations. First, "many
people who formerly engaged in magical practices became part of the
Ephesian church." Second, certain features of the spiritual environment,
which included magic, had an "incredibly strong pull . . . on believers."
He observes that it took God's sovereign intervention for converts "to
be sufficiently convicted that they should completely repent of their
ongoing utilization of amulets, charms, invocations, and traditional
means of gaining spiritual power."[37] He adds, "The connection of
Artemis to these magical practices is also borne out by the fact that she
is called upon repeatedly in the invocations of magical texts."[38]

Of the competing theories about the bulbous appendages on depictions of Artemis Ephesia, Arnold writes,

It may never be possible to retire her prevailing impression as a deity
with multiple breasts, and maternal properties, particularly in a

---

[37]Arnold, *Ephesians: Power and Magic*, 34.
[38]Arnold, *Ephesians: Power and Magic*, 35.

post-feminist era reviving (mistaken) notions of such a figure. Nor is the second leading modern theory, which argues for bull's scrota, likely to lose its sensational appeal.[39]

After working among the ruins and scholars at Ephesus, LiDonnici considers why such theories persist: "It is possible that the tendency to extend erotic category judgments to the art of antiquity makes it difficult for us to perceive a figure who is both unsexualized and at the same time fully gendered."[40]

THE "LEGS"

Images of the Ephesian Artemis from the waist down typically consist of tightly encased legs covered with images, most of which are wild beasts looking distressed, perhaps demonstrating the goddess's power over wildlife and nature.[41] The figures may even suggest power over evil spirits connected with these aspects of the natural world.

The legs are tightly swaddled, as if mummified. But one could see in them the body of a bee. Indeed, one of the images on the side of the statue's leg is a large bee (fig. 5.6), an insect which Morris says has had a long association with Ephesus, decorating its earliest coins.[42]

Several possibilities are put forth to explain the bee's meaning. In one version of a Greek bee story, Artemis's father, Zeus, was born in a cave, where bees protected him. Bees were also linked to the underworld, perhaps because

Figure 5.6. Bee imagery on front and side of Artemis of Ephesus (2nd century), Naples Archaeological Museum. Photo by Gary Glahn.

---

[39] Arnold, *Ephesians: Power and Magic*, 150.
[40] LiDonnici, "The Images," 411.
[41] LiDonnici, "The Images," 411.
[42] Morris, "Prehistoric Background," 139.

hives often appear in caves and crags—places seen as entrances to the underworld.

Artemis is associated with bee iconography elsewhere in the ancient world as well. Cook describes artifacts found in Rhodes; observing that among examples of primitive gold work, researchers found two oblong plaques embossed with the design of a winged female. From the waist down, this figure had "the body of a bee." He tells of similar pendants found in the same place that represent "the so-called Persic Artemis, a winged female with a lion on either side of her." He concludes that this Rhodes depiction of Artemis "affords some ground for taking" the figure in Ephesus "to be that of a bee-goddess, perhaps a bee-Artemis."[43]

Morris notes that the bee does enjoy a prehistoric role in early Anatolian myths. Seeing a great connection between Ephesus and Anatolia's elements of Hittite culture, she links Artemis's bee imagery not to Greek myth but to a Hittite one: that of Telipinu. In this story, the Hittite god Telipinu disappears and is brought back by a bee that purifies and overcomes where other gods have failed.[44]

Narrowing the focus from Anatolia to Ephesus itself, Immendörfer writes, "The Hittites were known for their bee keeping, and the bee always played an important role as a holy animal in the cult of the Ephesian goddess."[45]

Considering the connection between Artemis and bees, one may be tempted to see in Artemis a virgin queen bee representative of female power. But, to our knowledge, not until the 1600s did anyone know the

---

[43] Arthur B. Cook, "The Bee in Greek Mythology," *The Journal of Hellenic Studies* 15 (1895): 11. See also Hilda M. Ransome, *The Sacred Bee in Ancient Times and Folklore* (London: George Allen & Unwin, 1937), 84-135.

[44] Jared Aragona, trans., "The Myth of Telepinu, Hittite God of Fertility" (2021), https://open.maricopa.edu/worldmythologyvolume1godsandcreation/chapter/the-myth-of-telepinu-hittite-god-of-fertility.

[45] Immendörfer, *Ephesians and Artemis*, 87, citing a scholar, Burkert, who thinks Ephesus is identical with Apasa, capital of Arzawa, as described in Hittite sources. He adds that another source, Karwiese, claims it is possible to interpret an earlier iteration of the city's name as meaning "the city of the bee (goddess)."

queen bee was a she. An Amsterdam biologist dissected a honeybee and discovered the "king" bee possessed ovaries.[46] In the case of Artemis Ephesia, it seems more likely that the Hittite connection of bees with both magic and the underworld were the intent of the imagery.

Also possibly associated with the bee imagery is the honeycomb-like structure at Artemis's feet, as seen in figure 2.1.

CONCLUSION

Having considered the data, one can eliminate some theories, beginning with who Artemis was *not* in Paul's day. In Morford and Lenardon's *Classical Mythology*, the entry for Artemis includes a summary of what scholars know of the goddess from all sources.[47] In the book's broad sweep of Artemis, the authors make no association between the goddess and fertility, mothering, nurturing, or temple prostitution. Even beyond Ephesus, Artemis is associated with none of these qualities.

The various tools of analysis reveal that the data did not align with the fertility-related description of the goddess, whether from the first century or any other era, in Ephesus or beyond. The evidence is extensive enough to support the hypothesis that the Ephesians did not see Artemis as a mother or fertility goddess in Paul's day, if ever. Settlers who arrived more than a millennium before Paul might have found and accepted an Anatolian goddess whom they conflated with their own goddess, but Ephesians at the time of Paul worshiped a goddess they perceived as a female hunter who provided midwifery services while rejecting sexual relations.

One may wonder at the persistence, then, of the idea that Artemis was a mothering fertility goddess whose worshipers practiced temple prostitution. Baugh offers an explanation: "To prove the non-existence

---

[46]Frederique Lavoipierre, "Garden Allies: Honey Bees," Pacific Horticulture, www.pacifichorticulture
.org/articles/honey-bees. See also Harry B. Weiss, "Swammerdam, Jan Jacobz," *The Scientific Monthly*
25, no. 3 (Sept 1927): 220-27.

[47]Mark Morford and Robert Lenardon, *Classical Mythology* (New York: Oxford University Press,
2003), 117-19.

of something in antiquity requires direct and intimate familiarity with ancient people and societies and with ancient sources. It does not satisfy the skeptical reader to simply point out that no ancient sources exist which attest to the practice in that place or in that time."[48] As one who is familiar with the people, society, and sources, he writes, "Our conclusion will be that cult prostitution did not exist in Ephesus."[49] In this assertion his voice aligns with those of Oster, Trebilco, and Murphy-O'Connor, whom he says are quite correct in concluding that "sacred prostitution was never a Greek custom."[50] Baugh cites Oster as calling "the view of Artemis as a 'multibreasted fertility goddess' a 'gross misunderstanding' because of 'the paucity of ancient evidence that supports the idea.'"[51]

The architecture, sculptures, and coins relating to Artemis of the Ephesians align with the literary and epigraphic sources in supporting the narrative that people in Paul's day would have viewed Artemis Ephesia as the virgin daughter of Zeus and Leto, sister of Apollo, un-touchable by love, inactive sexually, and—although having strong local ties—worshiped throughout the empire. The data consistently point to Artemis of Ephesus as a traditional Greek goddess, "a virgin by choice, rejecting erotic dealings with males,"[52] though seemingly content with men's companionship.[53] She is also one who, while "inviolable" herself, "demands sexual purity of her followers."[54] Equipped with quiver and

---

[48]S. M. Baugh, "Cult Prostitution in New Testament Ephesus: A Reappraisal," *Journal of the Evangelical Theological Society* 42, no. 3 (September 1999): 444.

[49]Baugh, "Cult Prostitution," 444.

[50]Baugh, "Cult Prostitution," 447. About ten years after Baugh's article in which he added his voice to those of scholars concluding that sacred prostitution was never a Greek custom, Stephanie Budin published *The Myth of Sacred Prostitution in Antiquity* (New York: Cambridge University Press, 2008). The burden of proof appears to be on those who assert that such was the case. My findings align with those of Baugh, Oster, Trebilco, and Murphy-O'Connor. The assumption of rampant sacred prostitution is probably partially responsible for the persistence of the understanding of Artemis as a fertility goddess.

[51]Baugh, "Cult Prostitution," 425.

[52]Morford and Lenardon, *Classical Mythology*, 119.

[53]Artemis of the Ephesians had many male followers and was not a man hater. Numerous inscriptions were dedications by male devotees; see also the speech in Acts 19, especially verse 27.

[54]Morford and Lenardon, *Classical Mythology*, 119.

bow, accompanied by dogs, she hunts game. When humans are involved, her arrows can be painless if death is desired and ruthless if used as an executioner's tool. Artemis is easily offended, acts "swiftly and terribly," is "sensitive to cultic neglect,"[55] and seems to prefer female victims. Yet she can also choose to save.

So, although the Artemis Ephesia statue looks nothing like the image of the hunting Artemis, the story of her birth as part of the annual celebration in Ephesus connected the two. Brenk concludes, "Whatever the body language involved, both forms [of Artemis] apparently belonged to the same person, at least in the late Hellenistic and Roman period."[56] Neither a man hater nor a feminist as contemporary Westerners understand the words, Artemis was a virgin, and her priestesses and female cult leaders appear to have been sexually inactive.

Nevertheless, while the Ephesian version of Artemis seems to match Morford and Lenardon's description of the more generalized version of the goddess, she did take on additional emphases in Ephesus. Arnold says of Artemis Ephesia, "Her image adorned the coinage, a month of the year was named after her, Olympic-style games were held in her honor (called the Artemisia), and she was trusted as the guardian and protector of the city."[57] Sources dating to the imperial period describe corporate feasts, sacrifices, festivals, processions, contests, music, acting, magic, sacred games, and a birthday procession focused on the goddess's origin story. All of this suggests that she had a strong hold on the city of Ephesus.

As part of the goddess's ability to save, she was deemed one who could deliver a first-century female through the most dangerous of passages: childbirth. It might seem illogical to link celibacy with midwifery, but Homer's story of Artemis's birth provides the connection. In his version of the natal story, the goddess was the firstborn of twins,

---

[55]Morford and Lenardon, *Classical Mythology*, 118.
[56]Frederick E. Brenk, "Artemis of Ephesos: An *Avant Garde* Goddess," *Kernos* 11 (1998)· 157
[57]Arnold, *Ephesians: Power and Magic*, 31.

made her own birth painless for her mother, witnessed her mother's nine-day travail in delivering her brother, and determined to have nothing to do with sex or labor. Thus, from her nativity, Artemis was linked sympathetically with delivering another while never herself giving birth.

One might expect a goddess of midwifery to be associated only with saving and not both saving and killing. But in a sense, her killing can be seen as part of saving. This killing/saving connection makes more sense in view of the mortality rate in a world lacking analgesics, anesthetics, and C-sections. The pressure on the young to reproduce would have been great, and death frequently accompanied the experience. Knowing this, one can imagine how often a woman might utter the prayer, "Kill me painlessly with your arrows or deliver me—and my child—safely, but please don't leave me writhing for days like Leto birthing Apollo."

Artemis was worshiped as the protector, lord, preeminent god, and savior of the city of Ephesus. Cult statues communicated her power over both the natural and supernatural worlds in which humans could entreat her to work magic. What one does not find is a nurturing goddess of fertility. Again, the evidence suggests that Artemis of the Ephesians is nobody's mother.

6

SAVED THROUGH CHILDBEARING

THE GOAL OF CONSIDERING the identity of Artemis Ephesia at the time of the earliest Christians has been to provide a context for exploring the influence of the Artemis cult on Paul's first letter to Timothy—with particular focus on Paul's phrase "saved through childbearing" (1 Tim 2:15 NIV). Having used our tools of analysis—literary, epigraphic, architectural, and visual—we are better prepared to understand Paul's missive as his original readers might have.

BETTER THAN ARTEMIS

Artemis's main titles were listed previously as follows: first throne, queen, lord, savior, and god. Another was *manifest*. These are of particular interest when considering their overlap with titles Paul attributes to Christ in 1 Timothy. Four out of the six appear almost immediately in 1 Timothy 1, which has only twenty verses. *Manifest* appears in 1 Timothy 3.

One can find all of her titles in the Pauline corpus, but it appears that the apostle purposely loaded the introduction of this letter with titles for the true God that directly challenge Artemis without naming her directly.[1]

---

[1] It's worth noting that in 2 Timothy we find another of Artemis's seven key titles, this one relating to epiphany/appearance. Paul combines that title with that of Savior to describe the plan of God that has "now made visible through the **appearing of our Savior** Christ Jesus. He has broken the power of death and brought life and immortality to light through the gospel" (2 Tim 1:10).

Table 6.1. Titles of Artemis Compared with Pauline Titles for God in 1 Timothy

Regal (queen)	"Eternal King, Immortal" (1 Tim 1:17)
Lord	"Christ Jesus our Lord" (1 Tim 1:2)
Savior	"Savior" (1 Tim 1:1)
God	"God our Savior" (1 Tim 1:1); "God the Father" (1 Tim 1:2); "the blessed God" (1 Tim 1:11)

One might expect to find overlap in titles of gods, but what is unusual is Paul's use of four of the six right at the beginning, particularly since his doing so borrows from a vocabulary outside his norm. Paul usually refers to Jesus as "Christ Jesus," "Jesus Christ," "Christ," "the Lord," or "our Lord." Yet when writing to Timothy in Ephesus and Titus in Crete, Paul emphasizes the title "Savior." (Crete's goddess Britomartis—a virgin hunter and daughter of Zeus—was sometimes identified with the Greek Artemis.[2])

Paul's use of "Savior" is of particular interest because *TDNT* notes a "general restraint" for the use of "Savior" (*sōtēr*) in reference to God throughout the New Testament, in contrast to a "more common use [of the word] in the Pastorals." Three of the ten instances of *sōtēr* in the Pastorals are in 1 Timothy, and a fourth is in 2 Timothy. Interestingly, in 1 Timothy 4:10, *sōtēr* is used as a title. Contrast this with the rare later use of this word in the apostolic fathers.[3]

Considering that one of Artemis Ephesia's titles is *savior* and that Artemis wears Ephesus on her head in her role as the city's savior, perhaps Paul is emphasizing Jesus as Savior as a polemic against the false savior in Timothy's city. If so, Paul may also be hinting at the source of the false doctrine that is the object of his concern.

Paul's salutations to his recipients are listed below with titles of deity highlighted in bold for ease of reference. The reader will note that *savior* is not the title Paul usually uses (emphasis mine):

---

[2] Hesiod, *Theogony*, 474-79. As a reminder, Crete was home to the Curetes, who had a strong connection with Artemis Ephesia.

[3] *Theological Dictionary of the New Testament*, ed. Gerhard Kittel and Gerhard Friedrich, trans. Geoffrey W. Bromiley (Grand Rapids, MI: Eerdmans, 1964–1976), 1138-39.

- From Paul, a slave of Christ Jesus, called to be an apostle, set apart for the gospel of **God.** (Rom 1:1)

- From Paul, called to be an apostle of Christ Jesus by the will of **God,** and Sosthenes, our brother. (1 Cor 1:1)

- From Paul, an apostle of Christ Jesus by the will of **God,** and Timothy our brother, to the church of **God** that is in Corinth, with all the saints who are in all Achaia. (2 Cor 1:1)

- From Paul, an apostle (not from men, nor by human agency, but by Jesus Christ and **God the Father** who raised him from the dead). (Gal 1:1)

- From Paul, an apostle of Christ Jesus by the will of **God,** to the saints [in Ephesus], the faithful in Christ Jesus. (Eph 1:1)

- From Paul and Timothy, slaves of Christ Jesus, to all the saints in Christ Jesus who are in Philippi, with the overseers and deacons. (Phil 1:1)

- From Paul, an apostle of Christ Jesus by the will of **God,** and Timothy our brother, to the saints, the faithful brothers and sisters in Christ, at Colossae. Grace and peace to you from **God our Father!** (Col 1:1-2)

- From Paul and Silvanus and Timothy, to the church of the Thessalonians in **God the Father** and the Lord Jesus Christ. Grace and peace to you! (1 Thess 1:1)

- From Paul and Silvanus and Timothy, to the church of the Thessalonians in **God our Father** and the Lord Jesus Christ. Grace and peace to you from **God the Father** and the Lord Jesus Christ! (2 Thess 1:1-2)

- From Paul, a slave of **God** and apostle of Jesus Christ, to further the faith of God's chosen ones and the knowledge of the truth that is in keeping with godliness, in hope of eternal life, which **God,** who does not lie, promised before time began. But now in his own time he has made his message evident through the preaching I was entrusted with according to the command of **God our Savior**. To Titus, my genuine son in a common faith. Grace and peace from **God the Father** and **Christ Jesus our Savior**! (Titus 1:1-4)

- From Paul, a prisoner of Christ Jesus, and Timothy our brother, to Philemon, our dear friend and colaborer, to Apphia our sister, to Archippus our fellow soldier, and to the church that meets in your house. Grace and peace to you from **God our Father** and the Lord Jesus Christ! (Philem 1:1-3)

- From Paul, an apostle of Christ Jesus by the command of **God our Savior** and of Christ Jesus our hope, to Timothy, my genuine child in the faith. Grace, mercy, and peace from **God the Father** and **Christ Jesus our Lord**! (1 Tim 1:1-2)

- From Paul, an apostle of Christ Jesus by the will of **God**, to further the promise of life in Christ Jesus, to Timothy, my dear child. Grace, mercy, and peace from **God the Father** and **Christ Jesus our Lord**! (2 Tim 1:1-2)

Beyond the salutation differences, even though Paul does not usually use the word *savior* elsewhere, notice how often he uses it in correspondence with Titus/Crete and Timothy/Ephesians (emphasis mine):

- I was entrusted with according to the command of God our **Savior**. (Titus 1:3)

- Grace and peace from God the Father and Christ Jesus our **Savior**! (Titus 1:4)

- Showing all good faith, in order to bring credit to the teaching of God our **Savior** in everything. (Titus 2:10)

- As we wait for the happy fulfillment of our hope in the glorious appearing of our great God and **Savior**, Jesus Christ. (Titus 2:13)

- When the kindness of God our **Savior** and his love for mankind appeared. (Titus 3:4)

- Whom he poured out on us in full measure through Jesus Christ our **Savior**. (Titus 3:6)

- But our citizenship is in heaven—and we also await a **savior** from there, the Lord Jesus Christ. (Phil 3:20)

- Because the husband is the head of the wife as also Christ is the head of the church—he himself being the **savior** of the body. (Eph 5:23)

- From Paul, an apostle of Christ Jesus by the command of God our **Savior** and of Christ Jesus our hope. (1 Tim 1:1)

- Such prayer for all is good and welcomed before God our **Savior**. (1 Tim 2:3)

- In fact this is why we work hard and struggle, because we have set our hope on the living God, who is the **Savior** of all people, especially of believers. (1 Tim 4:10)

- But now **made visible** [manifest] through the appearing of our **Savior** Christ Jesus. He has broken the power of death and brought life and immortality to light through the gospel! (2 Tim 1:10)

Outside of writing to disciples in Crete and Ephesus, the apostle's letter to the Philippians includes the only Pauline reference to Christ as Savior.

In the same way that kryptonite evokes thoughts of Superman without uttering his name, Paul could refer to Jesus as *the/our Savior* in Ephesus and listeners would know he was exalting Christ over their local deity.

Michael Immendörfer, in *Ephesians and Artemis*, notes that Paul takes exactly such an approach in his letter to the Ephesians:

[Ephesians is] a theological masterpiece, which highlights the central importance of Artemis for Ephesus without naming the goddess *expressis verbis*, but which paraphrases her so clearly that the readers could know who (goddess) and what (cultic contents and activities) the author alluded to. He [Paul] adopts local Artemis terminology and redefines it in relation to Christ, so that cultic terms are used to criticize the cult . . . As readers were familiar with the [cult] language, it is very likely that they recognized the author's allusions and could comprehend the intended associations. They consist of direct attacks on the cult and of indirect polemic.[4]

One might wonder why Paul would want to avoid naming Artemis outright. Paul's Gentile traveling partner, Luke—presumably the author of Luke–Acts—directly names gods such as Artemis (Acts 19:24, 27-28, 34-35), Hermes (Acts 14:12), and Zeus (Acts 14:12-13). But the Jewish apostle Paul is never seen to use the proper name of any god but the God he worships. Instead, the apostle refers to other gods in round-about ways, such as "those who by nature are not gods" (Gal 4:8 NIV).[5] He infuses his missive with significance "christologically, without sliding into a syncretistic mixture."[6]

CONCERN ABOUT FALSE TEACHING

The first three verses of 1 Timothy reveal the broad purpose for Paul's letter. Having begun with reference to God as Savior (1 Tim 1:1), Paul tells Timothy his reason for leaving him in Ephesus: "As I urged you when I was leaving for Macedonia, stay on in Ephesus to instruct certain people not to spread false teachings" (1 Tim 1:3).

Recalling the circumstances under which Paul departed abruptly from Ephesus—the disturbance caused by Artemis's silversmiths

---

[4]Michael Immendörfer, *Ephesians and Artemis: The Cult of the Great Goddess of Ephesus as the Epistle's Context*, Wissenschaftliche Untersuchungen zum Neuen Testament II, Reihe 436 (Tübingen: Mohr Siebeck, 2017), 313.

[5]Consider what Paul says on the subject to the Corinthians: "We know that 'an idol in this world is nothing,' and that 'there is no God but one.' If after all there are so-called gods, whether in heaven or on earth (as there are many gods and many lords), yet for us there is one God, the Father, from whom are all things and for whom we live, and one Lord, Jesus Christ, through whom are all things and through whom we live" (1 Cor 8:4-6).

[6]The words Immendörfer (*Ephesians and Artemis*, 324) uses to describe Paul's approach in the book of Ephesians could be exactly applied to his approach in 1 Timothy.

(Acts 19)—one can see that the New Testament itself provides the context for why the threat to sound doctrine would have been on the author's mind. This threat was so great, it warranted stationing a teacher in the city with the express purpose of teaching others to stop spreading false doctrine.

While the NASB 1995 and NIV 1984 identify those teaching false doctrine as "men," Trombley points out that the Greek text uses a neuter pronoun, perhaps better translated "certain persons" or "some," thus allowing for both male and female teachers.[7] This detail is significant, as it opens the possibility that at least some teachers of falsehood in Ephesus are women.

Internal evidence supports such an idea. Paul describes young widows as "going around from house to house" (1 Tim 5:13). While one might envision female friends visiting in each other's living rooms, this phrase *house to house* describes how the church was meeting in Jerusalem (Acts 2:46; 5:42). If *house to house* is read as church gatherings, such a possibility might affect how we read both 1 Timothy 1:3 and 2 Timothy 3:6, which says some Ephesian heretics were sneaking their way "into households." Perhaps some young widows were teaching heresy from church gathering to church gathering.

Many come to the biblical text with the idea that women do not impart content; when this is the case, we don't picture them as operating in house churches and assume Paul is not including women among the false teachers in Ephesus. It's easy to interpret Paul as saying men are teaching false doctrine in church gatherings while women are "busybodies" in living rooms (1 Tim 5:13). More likely, though, both men and women in Ephesus were spreading false doctrine. And both men and women were believing lies.

Having reminded Timothy why he was stationed in Ephesus, Paul mentions mythology (1 Tim 1:4). In the next chapter he describes

---

[7]Charles Trombley, *Who Said Women Can't Teach?* (Gainesville, FL: Bridge-Logos, 1985), 185.

himself as called not to Jews but to the Gentiles (1 Tim 2:7). He expresses concern with issues relating to wives, remarriage, and multiple celibate women—that is, widows, young and old—in parts of 1 Timothy 2 and 5. The emphasis on celibacy in Ephesian religious contexts might account for the abundance of single women in the church in Timothy's care and suggest Gentiles are coming to faith from Artemis worship.

MAGIC AND OTHER ALLUSIONS TO ARTEMIS IN HER CITY

Some translations (including the CSB, ESV, NASB, NET, and NKJV) render Paul's description of the women as "gossips and busybodies" (1 Tim 5:13). Lloyd K. Pietersen writes, "Most consider this phrase as simply a stereotyping of women in much the same way as the author uses stereotypical language to describe his opponents." But Pietersen argues that one should instead translate *gossips* as "those who talk nonsense" and *busybodies* as "those who practi[c]e magic."[8] Pietersen thus helps readers connect the magic already seen in Acts (the magic-book-burning event) with what Paul would write later in his second missive to Timothy—namely, his mention of Jannes and Jambres (2 Tim 3:6-9).

The Old Testament never mentions Jannes and Jambres, but these men are listed in extrabiblical works[9] as being among the Egyptian magicians who opposed Moses.[10] When the author of Acts highlights

---

[8]See Lloyd K. Pietersen, "Women as Gossips and Busybodies? Another look at 1 Timothy 5:13," *Lexington Theological Quarterly* 42, no. 1 (Spring 2007): 19-35.

[9]"Jannes and Jambres, the legendary Egyptian magicians who opposed Moses and Aaron (Ex 7:11-22) and attracted considerable attention in late antiquity, have until recently been all but forgotten. Their names occur only once in the Bible (2 Tim 3:8), but Christian (e.g., Origen, Cyprian), Jewish (e.g., the Damascus Document, Targum Pseudo-Jonathan), and other (e.g., Pliny, Numenius) sources make it abundantly clear that stories about these men circulated widely and that a book recounting their exploits was well known by at least the third century CE. Not much of this has remained, however, and until the 1970s only a few lines of the book were known in Latin (published in 1861 by T. O. Cockayne and popularized by M. R. James in 1901)." See Michel Desjardins, "The Apocryphon of Jannes and Jambres the Magicians: P. Chester Beatty XVI," *The Journal of the American Oriental Society* 116, no. 3 (July–Sept 1996): 562.

[10]An apocryphal book, known as *The Apocryphon of Jannes and Jambres the Magicians*, exists in some Greek fragments present in the Chester Beatty Papyri no. XVI and in an extensive Ethiopic fragment

how magic has a grip on Ephesus (Acts 19:17-20), a form of the same word (*periergoi*, περίεργοι) often rendered as "busybodies" in translations of 1 Timothy 5:13[11] appears (*perierga*, περίεργα)—except that in Acts 19:19, it is translated as something like "magic arts." With this in mind, we read Paul's words about these men in his second letter to Timothy:

> For some of these insinuate themselves into households and captivate weak women who are overwhelmed with sins and led along by various passions. Such women are always seeking instruction, yet never able to arrive at a knowledge of the truth. And just as Jannes and Jambres opposed Moses, so these people—who have warped minds and are disqualified in the faith—also oppose the truth. But they will not go much further, for their foolishness will be obvious to everyone, just like it was with Jannes and Jambres. (2 Tim 3:6-9)

We have already seen the Artemis-magic connection. A few more inscriptions further validate the stronghold that magic had on Ephesus:

1. Three bear curses, one of which invokes Artemis to effect it.[12]

2. One fragment explicitly mentions a "magician" and two lines later connects the magician to Artemis through the genitive expression "of the goddess."[13]

3. A handful of inscriptions refer to the practices of divination, including one that refers to a "chief diviner."[14]

4. A gold magical amulet lists the cosmic powers of twenty-six Old Testament angels (thus probably reflecting Jewish magic).[15]

---

discovered in 2014. The *Testament of Solomon* (probably first century) also refers to the magicians by the name of Jannes and Jambres.

[11]See Pietersen, "Women as Gossips," 19-35.

[12]*IEph* 567-69; see especially no. 569 for the one invoking Artemis.

[13]*IEph* 3817A.

[14]*IEph* 1252; 1678; 1044.20.

[15]Clinton E. Arnold, *Ephesians: Power and Magic: The Concept of Power in Ephesians in Light of Its Historical Setting* (Grand Rapids, MI: Baker, 1992), 36.

The Roman government tried to forbid magic, including even the knowledge of it, according to Ingrid De Haas: "Throughout the Republic (510–27 BCE) and the Empire (27 BCE–CE 476) laws forbidding magic were enacted and practitioners and users of magic were persecuted and punished."[16] Vespasian (who ruled 69–79 CE) had outlawed astrology, too, but because of his friendship with a famous Ephesian astrologer, Balbilus, Vespasian let Ephesus continue holding sacred games in Balbilus's honor.[17] Balbilus spent his latter years in Ephesus, enjoying favors from Vespasian, who granted privileges to him and to Ephesus because of Balbilus's proficiency as an astrologer.[18] Also associated with magic in Ephesus were the *Ephésia grámmata*, or Ephesian letters. Apparently, these were well-known in southern Italy and Crete and dated to the late classical period. They were probably a corrupted form of the first line in hexameter of an early Greek incantation,[19] which people assumed had magical powers and used as part of charms and magic spells.

Beyond this workers-of-magic connection in 1 Timothy, one sees Paul making other veiled references to Artemis, her cult, and its context. To his recipient in a city known for its magnificent temple, Paul talks about the *living* pillar and base of truth (1 Tim 3:15). To Timothy in a place that loves the occult, he speaks of the devil's trap (1 Tim 3:7); describes the one made manifest as seen by angels (1 Tim 3:16); and warns of deceiving spirits (1 Tim 4:1), demonic teaching (1 Tim 4:1), and elect angels (1 Tim 5:21).

Where Artemis is esteemed as a light bearer, God "lives in unapproachable light" (1 Tim 6:16). Whereas inscriptions describe an Artemis-related mystery, Paul exclaims, "Great is the mystery of godliness" and "the mystery of our religion is great" (1 Tim 3:16 KJV,

---

[16]Ingrid De Haas, "Roman Magic: Control in an Uncertain World," The Ultimate History Project, https://ultimatehistoryproject.com/roman-magic-amulets-bullae-lunulae.html.

[17]Hans Willer Laale, *Ephesus (Ephesos): An Abbreviated History from Androclus to Constantine XI* (Nashville: Westbow Press, 2021), 250. Also see Matthew Bunsen, *Encyclopedia of the Roman Empire* (New York: Facts on File, 1994), 66.

[18]Laale, *Ephesus*, 52.

[19]D. R. Jordan, "A Love Charm with Verses," *Zeitschrift für Papyrologie und Epigraphik* 72 (1988): 245–59.

NRSV).[20] In a context where the goddess is *protos*, first and only, Paul says that God "alone possess immortality" (1 Tim 6:16). While Artemis is called a savior and deliverer, Paul calls Christ "the Savior of all" (1 Tim 4:10) and says wives will be saved through childbearing (1 Tim 2:15). And for women in a city that connects women's worship practices with wealth and social power, Paul charges Timothy to have godly women put off gold, pearls, braided hair, and fine apparel (1 Tim 2:9) and to instead adorn themselves with good deeds. In a city that connected religious positions with wealth, he wants overseers to be free from the love of money (1 Tim 3:3) and deacons not to be greedy (1 Tim 3:8). Rather than connecting godliness with profit, Christ-followers must connect their godliness with contentment (1 Tim 6:6), which brings profit of a different kind. Those who long to be rich are misguided (1 Tim 6:9), because "the love of money is the root of all evils" (1 Tim 6:10). Instead, the rich should hope not in riches, but in God, "who richly provides" (1 Tim 6:17).

Since one of the offices associated with Artemis's cult worship was for adorning the goddess, perhaps gold, pearls, and rich apparel were part of that emphasis. And if women held high-ranking public offices related to benefaction, one wonders if the church similarly enjoyed patronage by wealthy women. Jesus and his disciples had done so (Lk 8:1-3). Paul and many other believers elsewhere received benefaction from Phoebe (Rom 16:2). Financial support coming from wealthy women was part of early church practice, but that dynamic might have caused problems in a city where people connected spiritual practices with financial gain. Such a connection could be used to overpower others or leave one thinking autonomously rather than communally. Such a dynamic could explain why Paul wanted women in Ephesus to learn (1 Tim 2:11) rather than teach.

---

[20]The NET here (1 Tim 3:16) says, "Our religion contains amazing revelation," but adds this footnote: "*Grk* 'great is the mystery of [our] religion,' or 'great is the mystery of godliness.' The word 'mystery' denotes a secret previously hidden in God, but now revealed and made widely known."

TOO MANY CELIBATE WOMEN

Much of the context described here relates to women. And there's more. Virginity, celibacy, numerous widows and "forbidding to marry" (1 Tim 4:3 KJV) are also emphasized, both in inscriptions and in Paul's letter. He references single women who are young (1 Tim 5:11, 14), old (1 Tim 5:9), causing difficulty (1 Tim 5:15), and those encouraged to marry and have children (1 Tim 5:14).

Interestingly, when writing to the church in Corinth, where the church was dealing with sexual immorality (see 1 Cor 5–6), Paul gave the exact opposite advice that he gives to Timothy concerning single women. Paul wants Corinthian widows to consider remaining unmarried (1 Cor 7:8). But he wants younger Ephesian widows to marry and bear children (*teknogonein*, τεκνογονεῖν, 1 Tim 5:14). In expressing his wish for the latter, he uses a cognate of the same word in the verse that follows in the phrase "saved through childbearing" (*teknogonias*, τεκνογονίας, 1 Tim 2:15 NIV).

An understanding of the cultural background accounts for why the church in Ephesus had so many single women that the widows needed to be divided into three categories. A virgin goddess whose cult emphasized celibacy can easily account for many of the unique instructions in Paul's letter to Timothy.

"SAVED THROUGH CHILDBEARING" IN ITS CONTEXT

All of this prepares us to consider Paul's context when he talks about being "saved through childbearing." Here is the pericope once again:

> So I want the men [or husbands] to pray in every place, lifting up holy hands without anger or dispute. Likewise, the women [or wives] are to dress in suitable apparel, with modesty and self-control. Their adornment must not be with braided hair and gold or pearls or expensive clothing, but with good deeds, as is proper for women who profess reverence for God. Let a woman learn quietly with all submissiveness. But I am allowing a woman [or wife] neither to teach nor exercise [usurp? Have autonomous?] authority over a man [or husband]. She

must remain quiet. For Adam was formed first and then Eve. And Adam was not deceived, but the woman, because she was fully deceived, fell into transgression. But "she will be saved through [the] childbearing," if they continue in faith and love and holiness with self-control. This is a faithful saying. (1 Tim 2:8–3:1, author's translation)

Below, we will consider the above passage phrase by phrase. Cases in which the language of the translation seem wooden are my translations as I seek to highlight words and emphases.

So I want . . . (1 Tim 2:8)

The chapter begins with a *so* or *therefore*, linking what Paul has said with the action that should follow. And what has he just written? He wants all people to pray for kings and those in authority (1 Tim 2:2). Why? "That we may lead a peaceful and quiet life in all godliness and dignity" (1 Tim 2:2). Something was getting in the way of tranquility, and that needed to change for the sake of the gospel: "Such prayer for all is good and welcomed before God our Savior" (1 Tim 2:3). Why? "Since he wants all people to be saved and to come to a knowledge of the truth" (1 Tim 2:4). And why, according to Paul, would God want all to be saved and know the truth, as opposed to lies? Because he is the true God: "for there is one God" (1 Tim 2:5), as opposed to all others, who are false gods. And there is "one intermediary between God and humanity, Christ Jesus" (1 Tim 2:5)—not a member of the Gentiles' pantheon. This God was "himself human" (1 Tim 2:5), not made with hands like statues in the temple but made manifest in living and breathing human flesh. And what did this intermediary do? Instead of remaining only on the receiving end of sacrifices, which would be his right, he "gave himself as a ransom for all, revealing God's purpose at his appointed time" (1 Tim 2:6).

Paul goes on to tell what the nature of God in Christ has to do with the apostle's mission. He writes, "For this I was appointed a preacher and apostle—I am telling the truth; I am not lying—and a teacher of the Gentiles in faith and truth" (1 Tim 2:7). Paul roots his mission in

God's nature, as described to Timothy, in the context of ministry to Gentiles. All this Paul lays out as the rationale behind wanting everyone to pray. He returns to that thought and gives some advice:

> So I want the men [or husbands] in every place to pray, lifting up holy hands without anger or dispute. (1 Tim 2:8)

Anger and disputes were apparently getting in the way of the quietness needed for the gospel to thrive. This sex-specific (if translated as "men" or "women") or role-specific (if translated as "husbands" or "wives") instruction suggests that something about the group prayer time in Ephesus caused some males to lash out emotionally, resulting in arguments during worship.

> Likewise, the women [or wives] are to dress in suitable apparel, with modesty and self-control. Their adornment must not be with braided hair and gold or pearls or expensive clothing, but with good deeds, as is proper for women who profess reverence for God. (1 Tim 2:9-10)

And the females—what does Paul want from them? A certain kind of adornment. He is suggesting that the men (or husbands) were adorned with anger and disputing. The females, on the other hand, were adorned with emblems of their wealth.

Unfortunately, the idea that first-century pagans were obsessed with sex, especially as part of worship, has led scholars to see references to sex in texts where probably little to none was intended. The reference to modesty in 1 Tim 2:9 is one such place. Paul would have objected to sexually provocative apparel. But in this text in calling for modest dress, it appears he has social class in mind. Consider how Paul qualifies the sort of modesty he means: it is the opposite of braids, pearls, gold, and costly garments—all of which relate to socioeconomic status. These were associated with a person's rank. Additionally, other elements in the letter emphasize not problems of young women trying to attract men but their seeking to *avoid* attracting men, eschewing marriage (1 Tim 5:14).

Access to affordable costume jewelry and cubic zirconia, combined with the matronly images of pearl-draped icons like June Cleaver or the late Barbara Bush, make it difficult for many contemporary Western readers to imagine what a strong class statement a first-century woman would have made when she publicly displayed her dowry's worth of white beads. Pearls were the first-century woman's diamonds, and they were real. Pulitzer-winning author Stacy Schiff, in her biography *Cleopatra: A Life*, tells how Caesar once gifted his mistress a pearl worth the cumulative annual wages of 1,200 professional soldiers.[21] The cover of Schiff's book features Cleopatra's dark hair studded with pearls; it draws on the field of semiotics to create the suggestion that these gems were the first century's diamonds. Ephesus was a city on the Aegean Sea; it probably had a healthy trade in sea jewels, the ultimate of which were pearls.

Braids also made a class statement. For a woman to have a head full of fine locks wrapped in intricate creations required the luxuries of slave labor and leisure time. Bearing this in mind, a clearer picture of the author's intent emerges. To maintain such a style meant a woman belonged to the ruling or upper class, with the accompanying benefits of power and rank. Braids, pearls, and elaborate clothes reflected rank as much as wealth (compare Rev 18:16-17). Flaunting rank was not *modest*. Timothy opposed the wearing of such symbols in the place where Jew, Gentile, male, female, slave, and free worshiped together (compare Gal 3:27-29). Indications of rank had no place in the congregation of those who are interdependent.

Next, Paul mentions apparel. Lavish apparel had a long history in this city. Epigraphic evidence describes a legal case in the fourth century BCE in which forty-five inhabitants of nearby Sardis were sentenced to death for assaulting a sacred delegation dispatched from Ephesus to the shrine of Artemis in Sardis with tunics for the goddess.[22] Sokolowski notes that in addition to providing the first evidence of an Artemis Ephesia cult in Sardis, the discovery points to a practice of providing

---

[21]Stacy Schiff, *Cleopatra: A Life* (New York: Little, Brown, 2010), 39.
[22]*IEph.* 2, 334–300 BCE.

garments for Artemis's statue.[23] Closer to the time we are examining, we saw a religious office devoted to adorning Artemis. From all this, one might surmise that, as people tend to take on the characteristics of the gods or goddesses they follow, devotees of Artemis would have had reason to focus on rich apparel.

Fabric dealers in the Ephesian agora sold exquisite silks and woolens in a rainbow of colors, and if Artemis Ephesia's worshipers kept their statue clothed in great garments in Sardis, it seems likely that worshipers in Ephesus also would have kept the statue in their temple—the preeminent site for Artemis's worship—draped in dazzling fabrics.

Perhaps the practice of adorning Artemis was rooted in a statement in *The Iliad*, where Homer describes Artemis as "dressed in immortal garments" that included a "beautiful headband."[24] He also referred to the goddess as "gracefully arrayed."[25] Conceivably, the Ephesians sought to align their city's goddess with the vision of her that they inherited from antiquity.

A major source for information about Roman clothing is the monograph *Dress and the Roman Woman: Self-Presentation and Society.*[26] In it, Kelly Olson provides thorough information about Roman women's apparel, drawing on analysis of sculptures, inscriptions, coins, everyday wares, and wig fragments. Olson demonstrates that when the average Roman woman in antiquity stepped outside her home, her apparel and hairstyle would have conveyed visual signals about her rank (citizen, freeborn, slave), her marital status, in some cases her age, and even her moral status. Then and there, even more than here and now, dress meant representation. In the first-century province of Asia, hair, jewelry, and clothing revealed meaning beyond *who* people were; apparel and style communicated *whose* they were.

---

[23]F. Sokolowski, "A New Testimony on the Cult of Artemis of Ephesus," *Harvard Theological Review* 58, no. 4 (1965): 427-31.

[24]Homer, *The Iliad*, trans. E. V. Rieu (New York: Penguin, 2003), 21.505.

[25]Anonymous, "Hymn 27 to Artemis," *The Homeric Hymns and Homerica*, trans. Hugh G. Evelyn-White (Cambridge, MA: Harvard University Press, 1914), 14.

[26]Kelly Olson, *Dress and the Roman Woman: Self-Presentation and Society* (New York: Routledge, 2008).

Ethicist Steven Inrig has noted that the vision presented in 1 Timothy aligns with Paul's vision elsewhere of a community devoid of rank, one that "actively works to ease or erase separations based on class and power." In such a gathering, "a slave could be an elder over a master, [and] clothing among men and women could subvert and reinscribe social demarcations of power, class, and worth. In such gatherings the poor or slaves would enter feeling welcome, as their appearance lacked the usual markings that revealed their rank in the social hierarchy."[27] Indeed, in such a place a slave could become a bishop, and a paterfamilias would wash a slave's feet.

While one mark of those driven by love is that they refrain from dressing in a sexually provocative way, seeing only sexual purity in the admonition to dress modestly loses something of the vision the author of 1 Timothy would have had for a Christ-honoring fellowship. An understanding of the city's most influential pagan influence, Artemis, and how the author related to the goddess's cult can help today's readers gain a clearer sense of the kind of radical, countercultural fellowship he intended Christ's church to be.

Before looking at specific words in verse 11, it's important to consider the verse as a whole:

> Let a woman learn quietly with all submissiveness. (1 Tim 2:11 ESV)

The imperative here is to let her learn: let a woman in quietness learn with all submissiveness. Twice Paul stresses the way she learns, suggesting that whereas men (or husbands) were angry, unlearned women (or wives) needed to quiet down in learning contexts. Having seen this, we consider some specifics.

> Let a woman . . . (1 Tim 2:11)

Koine Greek has only one word for *woman* or *wife*, (*gynē*, γυνή). The same is true of *man* and *husband* (*anēr*, ἀνήρ). Context determines

---

which the writer intends, but when the two appear together, they almost always mean married people. A Christian woman with a man at home is a wife (1 Cor 14:35). More relevant to this passage, one would expect that in Paul's mind, a Christian woman experiencing child-bearing would be a wife (1 Tim 2:15).

Most contemporary translators have rendered *gynē* here as the universal—and thus more broad-sweeping—"woman." The difference in interpretation amounts to the difference between telling *some wives* they need to stop making the learning environment contentious versus telling *all women* they can never teach. Since the advent of second-wave feminism, most of the newer translations (such as the NASB, earlier editions of the NIV, and the ESV) are actually *more* restrictive in application than earlier translations.

The presence of the word *childbearing* later in the pericope suggests that the more limited "wife" would be the better translation of *gynē*, and with it the corresponding "husband" instead of "man."

Some argue against "wife," noting that the author's appeal to modesty earlier in the context would extend to all women, not just wives. It's true that all women—not only the married—would need to be modest. But when one considers that the average female married in her teens and that *modesty* here was probably concerned with class distinctions, it seems doubtful that Paul is enjoining young girls to put away flashy jewelry. Instead, he is probably more focused on people with a greater degree of agency over how they present themselves—wives.

Yet why would Paul want to limit any females at all, even a smaller subset of women? In his work *Roman Wives, Roman Widows*, Bruce Winter offers a possible motivation. He points to aspects of Roman law that regulated behavior patterns, concluding, "Some of the instructions to the Pauline communities appear to have been framed, taking cognizance of those laws."[28] Elsewhere Winter elaborates on the laws to

---

[28] Bruce Winter, *Roman Wives, Roman Widows* (Grand Rapids, MI: Eerdmans, 2003), 3.

which he is referring: "Women were not to intervene (*intercede*) in public settings nor come between two parties, and an imperial ban already existed from the time of Augustus on women intervening on behalf of their husbands in the context of legal argument."[29]

If one imagines a home assembly, before the advent of church buildings, and replaces a pulpit-preaching time with group exhortations, it becomes easier to see how some might view a public husband-wife interaction. Especially if a wife scrutinized her husband's prophecies, outsiders could view her actions as violating civil law. If we recall that Ephesus was the provincial capital from the time of Augustus and that the city of Ephesus served as a port for exporting the Christian message to the rest of the empire, we can better understand why the good reputation of the Christian assembly in the community here would have been especially important.

An internal-evidence factor argues further for readers to view the text in question as referring only to wives. Elsewhere, Peter gives instruction specifically directed to wives. When compared with the instructions in 1 Timothy, we see that the two passages have astonishing similarities, perhaps due to a preformed tradition.

Table 6.2. "Women" or "Wives"?

1 Peter 3:3-6 (definitely "wives")	1 Timothy 2:9-13 ("women" or "wives"?)
Adornment (1 Pet 3:3), adorned (1 Pet 3:5)	Adornment (1 Tim 2:9)
Braiding of hair (1 Pet 3:3)	Braided hair (1 Tim 2:9)
Gold jewelry (1 Pet 3:3)	Gold or pearls (1 Tim 2:9)
Fine clothes (1 Pet 3:3)	Expensive clothing (1 Tim 2:9)
Pure, reverent (1 Pet 3:2)	Modesty, self-control (1 Tim 2:9)
Tranquil (1 Pet 3:4)	Quietly (1 Tim 2:11), quiet (1 Tim 2:12)
Being subject (1 Pet 3:5)	All submissiveness (1 Tim 2:11)
Let . . . not be (1 Pet 3:3)	I do not allow (1 Tim 2:12)
Sarah and Abraham (1 Pet 3:6)	Adam then Eve (1 Tim 2:13)
Husband (own husbands, their husbands) (1 Pet 3:1, 5)	Man/husband (1 Tim 2:12)

---

[29]Winter, *Roman Wives*, 93.

Observing these great similarities, George and Dora Winston con-clude, "It would seem that there was a common underlying apostolic teaching based on Genesis concerning the relationship of wives to hus-bands, reflected here by both Peter and Paul."[30]

Today, Protestants tend to expect married women, especially if married to pastors, to have more freedom to engage in public ministries in the church than do single women. But before the Protestant Refor-mation, the opposite was true. Part of earlier church thinking about single women (later, nuns) was that a virgin or widow (a without-a-man woman, in its broadest definition) was freer to minister than a married woman, and thus more likely to teach.

Having considered some of the details, we return to the overall concept Paul is communicating. The translation here is inelegant, but it allows the reader to see the word order and the subtle stress on learning:

> A woman (or wife) in quietness let learn with all submissiveness.
> (1 Tim 2:11, author's translation)

As noted above, "Let a woman (or wife) learn" is the only imperative in the passage. Sometimes a translation buries the imperative. And readers may also miss its significance by focusing only on the limitation that follows. In the context of biblical instruction, women had often been excluded from public learning contexts—but Paul insists that they be allowed to learn.

He also sets forth the manner in which he wants them to learn. The word for *quietly* here is not a reference to absolute silence. Paul uses a form of *quietness* three times in his argument: he starts by saying he wants prayer for government leaders, so the believer can live a peaceful and *quiet* life (1 Tim 2:2); then twice he stresses the demeanor he wants learning women (or wives) to have (1 Tim 2:11-12). The preposition *in*

---

[30]George Winston and Dora Winston, *Recovering Biblical Ministry by Women* (Longwood, FL: Xulon Press, 2003), 113.

appears in these latter two references—so, "in quietness." That Paul emphasizes this quality suggests the opposite was happening, perhaps as a response to the men's (or husbands') anger and disputing (1 Tim 2:8). Some translators have rendered the word *quiet* as "settle down" in other passages (2 Thess 3:12 NIV). So, when it comes to these women learning, we can better understand the author's intention if we bear in mind that the quiet to which he is referring is the same quiet in which he called all to live (1 Tim 2:2).

Consider the difference in his writing to Timothy, "I am allowing a woman neither to teach nor to . . . ," versus writing to a church saying, "Women are not to teach men." One states his practice to an individual; the other suggests a principle.

> I am allowing a woman [or wife] neither to teach nor to exercise authority over a man [or husband]. (1 Tim 2:12, author's translation)

In saying "I suffer not" (KJV) or, in contemporary terms, "I do not allow," Paul uses the present tense, which in Greek has more of a sense of progressive action than in English. So a first-century Koine-speaking person would probably have heard this phrase to mean, "I am not allowing." Reading "I'm not allowing" as a progressive statement emphasizes the idea that *disallowing* is the practice of this particular author. That differs from a directive or command, and it also suggests he did not necessarily intend for his instruction to stand for all people, in all places, and for all time. He's laying out what he himself does not do, not necessarily proclaiming, "Thus sayeth the Lord."

Not all present-tense verbs are to be understood this way. But what gives this possibility more credibility is the addition of a first-person pronoun: "*I* am not allowing." As mentioned, one sees similar first-person language elsewhere when the apostle Paul refers to the unmarried. In his instructions for the Corinthians regarding virgins, he writes that "I have no command from the Lord, but I give my opinion as one shown mercy by the Lord to be trustworthy" (1 Cor 7:25).

Perhaps one should conclude that when it came to women, wives, marriage, and teaching, Paul saw himself as speaking wisdom for specific circumstances rather than making decrees for all people, for all time.

Looking back at the text at hand, we see how different translators have rendered 1 Timothy 2:12:

> "But I suffer not a woman to teach, nor to usurp authority over the man, but to be in silence." (KJV)

> "I do not permit a woman to teach or to assume authority over a man; she must be quiet." (NIV)

> "But I do not allow a woman to teach or to exercise authority over a man, but to remain quiet." (NASB)

> "And I do not permit a woman to teach or to have authority over a man, but to be in silence." (NKJV)

Interestingly, some recent English translations are more conservative, or limiting to women, in how they render texts that talk about women—especially this passage. Note once again that the oldest translation, the KJV, disallows *usurping* authority, whereas later versions disallow even the possession or exercise of authority. In rendering the text this way, the later translators suggest that Timothy's mentor intended only men, not women, to teach in settings with men present.

New Testament scholar Philip Payne questions whether Paul has two prohibitions in mind here, both teaching and exercising authority. He takes the two ideas as one in the same way an American might say "I'm sick and tired" to mean "I'm weary." Payne suggests that the author has only one limitation in mind—to disallow those who teach in such a way that they usurp authority. Payne writes, "Paul typically uses οὐδέ to convey a single idea, as do the two closest syntactical parallels to 1 Tim 2.12 ["teach" and "exercise/usurp authority"]." Payne observes that in the overwhelming majority of Paul's and the New Testament's "neither . . . nor . . . but" syntactical constructions, οὐδέ joins two expressions to convey a single idea in sharp contrast to the following ἀλλά statement.[31] So he sees historical precedent for treating teaching and authority as a single prohibition ("women teaching with self-assumed authority over a man").[32]

In contrast, Schreiner and Köstenberger view the more conservative translations as offering needed correctives. These scholars argue that the conjunction in "neither to teach *nor* to exercise authority" pairs two synonyms, asserting that Paul's pairing required both to be read as positive or both as negative, but not one positive and one negative. Since teaching is generally positive, they deduce that the kind of authority intended must also be good—not "usurping," which is negative.

The problem with the latter analysis, according to Linda L. Belleville, is that the two infinitives involved, "to teach" and "to have authority" or "to usurp authority," function grammatically "not as verbs but as nouns in the sentence structure."[33] By expanding surveys of word usage to include pairings of nouns and noun substitutes, she says, one finds ancient writers using such constructions to express a goal or purpose.

If Payne and Belleville are correct, a translation might be, "I am not permitting a wife to teach *with a view to* domineering a husband, but to be in quietness" (1 Tim 2:12, emphasis added). If so, the author's instruction suggests that both husbands and wives in the assembly need to calm down. The men/husbands are angry during prayer, and the women/wives are acting in a way that communicates a sense of superiority or perhaps violates civil law.

A study of the word *authentein*, translated here as "authority," is of little help. Whether Paul had in mind to "exercise authority" or "usurp authority" is unclear from the word itself. That is why translators resort

---

[31]Philip Payne, "1 Tim 2.12 and the Use of οὐδέ to Combine Two Elements to Express a Single Idea," *New Testament Studies* 54, no. 2 (2008): 235-53.
[32]Payne, "Single Idea," 253.
[33]Linda L. Belleville, "Teaching and Usurping Authority," in *Discovering Biblical Equality*, 2nd ed., ed. Ronald W. Pierce and Rebecca Merrill Groothuis (Downers Grove, IL: InterVarsity Press, 2004), 217.

to grammar for validation. The word Paul has chosen differs from the common word for authority (*exousia*); in fact, *authentein* is a *hapax legomenon*, so we can't study its use elsewhere in the New Testament.

Nevertheless, writers used *authentein* outside of the New Testament. Sometimes, though not always, the word had nuances as negative as *murder*. First-century authors used a form of the word to refer to "those who rule, to dominating masters, or to autocrats"; "one who dominates"; and "someone who prevailed or compelled."[34] The uses in extrabiblical literature lend weight to the assertion that the very structure of the sentence weights it toward meaning "to teach in such a way as to usurp authority." It makes better sense of both the immediate context and the entire canon of Scripture to understand the author as prohibiting a certain kind of teaching—a negative kind.

Whether Paul intended to limit one kind of action (teaching a certain way) or two (teaching and acting autonomously), he was addressing a specific time-bound situation: both men and women (or husbands and wives) in the assembly at Ephesus needed to stop doing something disruptive. Men, or a specific subset of them, were angry during the assembly, and women, or a specific subset of them, were disrupting worship.

Once again, Ephesian culture might shed light on Paul's meaning here—namely, the real-and-not-mythological Amazons and their independence from men. They did not hate men. But they remained unmarried, raised daughters without fathers, and were characterized by autonomy from males. Their connection to Artemis in Ephesus is well established by the city's origin story, as seen in places such as public stone reliefs and temple statues of Amazons, and in multiple mentions of them in the literature.

---

[34]For an excellent brief analysis of the word and its use, see Jamin Hübner, "Revisiting αὐθεντέω in 1 Timothy 2:12: What Do the Extant Data Really Show?," *Journal for the Study of Paul and His Letters* 5, no. 1 (Summer 2015): 41-70. See also chapters eight and nine of Cynthia Long Westfall, *Paul and Gender: Reclaiming the Apostle's Vision for Men and Women in Christ* (Grand Rapids, MI: Baker Academic, 2016).

Paul appears to have a habit of alluding to Artemis meanings, so one wonders if he might have done so here in his word choice. *Authentein* is an unusual word to use if he simply means "to have" or "to exercise authority," but it's entirely possible the word he does use would evoke autonomy. The word *over* (that is, over a man/husband) is not in the text. *Authentein* is an infinitive. Its range of meaning includes acting with autonomy or independently. In some contexts, autonomy and independence are good, but Paul seems to prefer interdependence when talking about male-female relations: "In the Lord woman is not independent of man, nor is man independent of woman. For just as woman came from man, so man comes through woman. But all things come from God" (1 Cor 11:11-12). He wrote these words to the Corinthians probably while he was in Ephesus.

> She must remain quiet. (1 Tim 2:12)

Paul reiterates his point, bookending his call for quiet on the part of women. Earlier he said quiet lives were essential to the gospel. Elsewhere, he told the Thessalonians to aspire to live a quiet life (1 Thess 4:11). The quietness he references is required of all Christians to please God and provide the greatest credibility for the gospel. Apparently, the men (or husbands) in Timothy's context were the opposite in how they were expressing their anger, which they needed to replace with a different kind of words: prayer (1 Tim 2:8). After establishing this, Paul enjoins the women (or wives) specifically in worship gatherings to stop the disruption. Women were to learn and refrain from teaching men (or husbands) and replace disruptive words with quietness.

Why? Paul gives his rationale:

> For Adam was formed first and then Eve. And Adam was not deceived, but the woman, because she was fully deceived, fell into transgression. But she will be saved through [the] childbearing, if they continue in faith and love and holiness with self-control. (1 Tim 2:13-15)

The statement in 1 Timothy that "she will be saved through [the] child-bearing, if they . . ." comes near the end of a pericope in which Paul has said he is allowing a woman (or wife) neither to teach nor *authentein* a man (1 Tim 2:12). He offers two reasons for his practice: (1) The woman, not the man, was the one deceived and (2) Adam was formed first. These rationales he follows with a consolation that "she will be saved through [the] childbearing, if . . ."

Some understand Paul's reasoning in 1 Timothy 2 to be "rooted in the created order."[35] They see the apostle as saying the practice he disallows is for all time because his reasons draw on a prefall reality. Consequently, the prohibition is based on a "principle of male headship," a concept derived from Adam being first, which for many equates to hierarchy.[36]

As was established earlier, the traditional view of the church has been that Paul's reason for limiting women's speech is because women are more easily deceived than men. But more recently, the rationale has shifted from Eve's deception—extrapolated to all women—to the creation order of Adam and Eve, with Adam—the first—being preeminent.[37]

But "Adam was formed first . . . not deceived" should not be under-stood as a male-first creation order that equals hierarchy, either in this world or the next. Rather, the truths that "Adam was first" and "Eve was deceived" restore interdependence in a context in which pride of creation order in a goddess-first context emphasizes preeminence and autonomy. In the Ephesian origin story, Artemis is first; it's one of her titles. In her own creation story, with its female-male pairing, she is firstborn.

---

[35] For example, Thomas Schreiner in *Recovering Biblical Manhood and Womanhood: A Response to Evangelical Feminism*, ed. John Piper and Wayne Grudem (Wheaton, IL: Crossway, 2021), 239. Schreiner citing Philip Towner, 239; Dorothy Patterson, 335.

[36] Schreiner, *RBMW*, 232. Also, "The priority of Adam in creation would have naturally suggested his authority over Eve to the original readers. Paul does not endorse primogeniture per se in 1 Timothy 2:13; he appeals to the creation of Adam first in explaining why women should not teach men" (235).

[37] See William G. Witt, "The Argument 'from Tradition' Is Not the 'Traditional' Argument," in *Icons of Christ: A Biblical and Systematic Theology for Women's Ordination* (Waco, TX: Baylor University Press, 2020), 19-41.

Paul's Lord was begotten, not created, and firstborn over all creation, so there is no parallel creation story of his beginning. But in the creation of humanity, the Genesis story, the man is first in a male-female pairing—and he was not even the one deceived. The apostle corrects a false story with a true one. He is using a narrative to counter a competing narrative.

He is not saying women are more deceived than men. Scripture teaches that women and men are both vulnerable to deception. Paul himself wrote to the Corinthians, "I am afraid that just as the serpent deceived Eve by his treachery, your minds may be led astray from a sincere and pure devotion to Christ" (2 Cor 11:3). Male-female differences in levels of deception are not due to ontology or biology but rather to differences in age, education, experience, and opportunity. If women as a class were more easily deceived than men, Paul would not have women instructing children, the most vulnerable of all humans.

While scholars vary in their understanding of Paul's two reasons for limiting women (Eve's deception, and creation order), they also vary in their interpretation of Paul's consolation, the assurance about being "saved through childbearing" (1 Tim 2:15 ESV).

> But she will be saved through [the] childbearing, if they continue in faith and love and holiness with self-control. This is a faithful saying. (1 Tim 2:15–3:1)

How interesting that Paul brings up deliverance through childbirth in a context where false teaching is likely coming from the cult of the goddess of midwifery—especially because he is bringing up a creation story to counter beliefs in a city that prides itself in its goddess's birth.

Eve's consequence was pain in childbearing. Artemis was thought to deliver painlessly or euthanize women in childbirth. But Jesus is better. He will save through childbearing those who continue in faith, love, and holiness with self-control.

But what exactly does Paul mean by *save*? To help determine how Timothy would have read Paul's use of *save* here, we'll consider Paul's use of the same tense (future, active indicative) of *save* elsewhere in his writings, and then we'll look at this form of *save* in broader New Testament usage.[38] Here are the Pauline uses of "will be saved" in the New Testament. Italics are part of the cited translation referencing Old Testament quotes, so bold has been added to the phrase "will be saved" in each verse below for easy identification:

And Isaiah cries out on behalf of Israel, "*Though the number of the children of Israel are as the sand of the sea, only the remnant* **will be saved**." (Rom 9:27)

For *everyone who calls on the name of the Lord* **will be saved**. (Rom 10:13)

And so all Israel **will be saved,** as it is written: "*The Deliverer will come out of Zion; he will remove ungodliness from Jacob*." (Rom 11:26)

If someone's work is burned up, he will suffer loss. He himself **will be saved,** but only as through fire. (1 Cor 3:15)

But she **will be delivered** through childbearing, if she continues in faith and love and holiness with self-control. (1 Tim 2:15)

Here are verses that contain the same form of "will be saved" as above, only in broader New Testament usage:

And you will be hated by everyone because of my name. But the one who endures to the end **will be saved**! (Mt 10:22)

But the person who endures to the end **will be saved**. (Mt 24:13)

You will be hated by everyone because of my name. But the one who endures to the end **will be saved**. (Mk 13:13)

The one who believes and is baptized **will be saved,** but the one who does not believe will be condemned. (Mk 16:16)

---

[38]In Pauline use: Rom 9:27; 10:13; 11:26; 1 Cor 3:15; 1 Tim 2:15. In the rest of the New Testament: Mt 10:22; 24:13; Mk 13:13; 16:16; Lk 8:50; Jn 10:9; 11:12; Acts 2:21.

But when Jesus heard this, he told him, "Do not be afraid; just believe, and she **will be healed**." (Lk 8:50)

I am the door. If anyone enters through me, he **will be saved**, and will come in and go out, and find pasture. (Jn 10:9)

Then the disciples replied, "Lord, if he has fallen asleep, he **will recover**." (Jn 11:12)

And then everyone who calls on the name of the Lord ***will be saved***. (Acts 2:21)

In the above examples, one can see that "will be saved" has to do with eternal or physical salvation, not maturing in character. Nor does it refer to role fulfillment. Rather, in every case in which New Testament writers used the future active indicative for *save*, the term refers to eternal salvation or physical deliverance.

The plainest reading of "will be saved through childbearing" would be to understand Paul as saying that "she will be saved" refers to salvation from the eternal judgment of God. Consequently, some do think that "a woman will be saved through childbearing" refers to women being exempt from God's eternal judgment through having children. Maretha M. Jacobs, speaking of 1 Timothy 2:15, writes, "Salvation, according to the author of this letter, seemingly comes differently, even conditionally for women." She says some think the reference to childbearing means "women can 'earn' their salvation by bearing children."[39]

Indeed, one might conclude that Paul is saying that women who give birth will be granted entrance into heaven. Such an idea contradicts both all other Pauline teaching on the subject and the entire story of Scripture and its teaching about salvation by grace through faith (Titus 3:7; Eph 2:8-9; along with the entire argument of the book

---

[39]Maretha M. Jacobs, "On Fairness and Accuracy in the Academy: A Brief Response to Wim Vergeer's Use of Terminologies, and Some Simplifications, in the Article 'The Redeemer in an "Irredeemable Text" (1 Tim. 2:9-15),'" *Neotestamentica* 51, no. 2 (2017): 362.

of Romans). Timothy would have been familiar with Paul's teaching on salvation by grace through faith for eternal salvation. Notably, the spiritual destiny of women is not even the topic Paul is addressing either in 1 Timothy overall nor in the immediate context. Additionally, if Paul believed all women needed to give birth, he would not have written elsewhere that some women should remain single (see 1 Cor 7:8).

To see *saved* as a reference to eternal salvation is to read the words in the text most plainly. And as one of my hermeneutics professors said, "When the plain sense of the text makes sense, seek no other sense." Yet such a reading *doesn't* make sense. So conversely, when the plain sense of the text makes little sense, we should seek another sense.

A LOCAL SAYING?

If we entertain the possibility that "saved through childbearing" refers not to eternal life but to temporal deliverance—saved from dying in childbirth—we can address another question. What if the author was assuring Timothy that, in light of the nature of the local false deity, a woman in his pastoral care would not die in childbirth? That is, assuming a woman trusted in the *true* Savior and Deliverer—and assuming she had the character-qualifying standards of faith, charity, holiness, and sobriety—she would be delivered by a different Deliverer. This is not to suggest Paul is making a universal statement that would be true of all women in all eras. Rather, it would be true in the case of Timothy and his congregation in the short term, a promise that in this foundational period of their assembly, their God would prove himself bigger than the god of the surrounding culture.

The fact that the writer changes from singular to plural in the same sentence ("she will be saved if they. . . ."), violating a rule of grammar to do so, provides a hint that he may be borrowing a local quote. That is, part of his statement could be quoted material: "and 'she will be saved in childbearing.'" Then he tacks on the qualifications ("if") and then ends with the phrase, "*This* is a faithful saying." The latter suggests he may have in mind a popular saying that he's co-opting for his own purposes. Interestingly, the Greek/English diglot of the NET attaches a footnote to this childbearing verse: "The verse may point to some sort of proverbial expression now lost, in which 'saved' means 'delivered.'"[40]

Paul borrowed local sayings with some regularity. Scholars have identified the following phrases as examples. I have included my own translation of 1 Timothy 2:15–3:1 to offer what I consider a more precise rendering. In every case but one (1 Cor 6:12, where the quotation marks were already part of the translation), I have added quotation marks to identify what scholars believe is quoted material. Italicized words below are part of the translation text, so for emphasis I have added bold type to indicate where the saying ends and is followed by a contrastive qualification.

"All things are lawful for me"—**but** not everything is beneficial. "All things are lawful for me"—**but** I will not be controlled by anything. (1 Cor 6:12)

Now with regard to the issues you wrote about: "It is good for a man not to have sexual relations with a woman." **But** because of immoralities, each man should have relations with his own wife and each woman with her own husband. (1 Cor 7:1-2)

Flee sexual immorality! "Every sin a person commits is outside of the body"—**but** the immoral person sins against his own body. (1 Cor 6:18)

But "she will be saved through childbearing" **if** they continue in faith and love and sanctity with self-restraint. This saying is trustworthy. (1 Tim 2:15–3:1, author's translation)

For "bodily discipline is only of little profit," **but** godliness is profitable for all things, since it holds promise for the present life and *also* for the *life* to come. It is a trustworthy statement deserving full

[40]Glahn, Sandra L., "The First-Century Ephesian Artemis: Ramifications of Her Identity," *Bibliotheca Sacra* 172, no. 688 (October–December 2015): 468. See NET Bible, 1 Tim 2:15, footnote 24.

acceptance. (1 Tim 4:8-9 NASB1995; italics original, quotation marks mine)[41]

In addition to using quoted material followed by his own Christianized twist, Paul sometimes adds the phrase, "This is a faithful saying," to amplify or clarify a truth to be emphasized. One cannot help but notice that these faithful sayings tend to appear in the same context with the word or idea of *save* (emphasis mine):

This saying is trustworthy and deserves full acceptance: "Christ Jesus came into the world to **save** sinners"—and I am the worst of them! (1 Tim 1:15)

This saying is trustworthy:

> If we died with him, we will also **live with him**.
> If we endure, we will also **reign with him**.
> If we deny him, he will also deny us.
> If we are unfaithful, he remains faithful, since he cannot deny himself. (2 Tim 2:11-13)

But "when the kindness of God our **Savior** and his love for mankind appeared, he **saved** us not by works of righteousness that we have done but on the basis of his mercy, through the washing of the new birth and the renewing of the Holy Spirit, whom he poured out on us in full measure through Jesus Christ our **Savior**. And so, since we have been justified by his grace, we become heirs with the confident expectation of eternal life." This saying is trustworthy. (Titus 3:4-8)

And possibly:

Notwithstanding she shall be **saved** in childbearing, if they continue in faith and charity and holiness with sobriety. This is a true saying. (1 Tim 2:15–3:1 KJV)[42]

---

[41] The NET makes the contrast less obvious here: "For 'physical exercise has some value, but godliness is valuable in every way. It holds promise for the present life and for the life to come.' This saying is trustworthy and deserves full acceptance" (1 Tim 4:8-9).

[42] The NET renders the word *saved* as *delivered* here.

It is worth noting that most English translations of 1 Timothy 3:1 place the phrase "this is a faithful saying" at the beginning of a new paragraph following the mention of childbirth, thus interpreting the phrase as referring to what follows: "This saying is trustworthy: 'If someone aspires to the office of overseer . . .'"

But the saying may precede the statement—that is, the statement may refer back to childbearing. Sometimes the phrase "this is a faithful saying" precedes the saying it references; sometimes it follows the saying. Note the difference in meaning, depending on where the comment about the faithful saying goes:

> But [she] will be saved through childbearing—if they continue in faith, love and holiness with propriety. Here is a trustworthy saying.
>
> Whoever aspires to be an overseer desires a noble task.

> But [she] will be saved through childbearing—if they continue in faith, love and holiness with propriety.
>
> Here is a trustworthy saying: Whoever aspires to be an overseer desires a noble task.[43] (1 Tim 2:15–3:1)

In the first option above, the phrase "here is a trustworthy saying" stays with the preceding paragraph, which is how the NET diglot shows it in the Greek text—and how John Chrysostom, in the fourth century, understood its placement.[44] In this reading, the saying refers to being saved through childbearing rather than aspiring to be an overseer. In the second option, "this is a faithful saying" begins new paragraph. This layout is how most English translations separate chapters 2 and 3. In such a reading, the saying relates to being an elder.

The difference is relevant because it leaves open the possibility that Paul was quoting a saying known to his readers that related to

---

[43]The NIV adds no female pronouns in 1 Timothy 2:15, which is the reason I use it here with a bracketed change to reflect the singular in the Greek.

[44]John Chrysostom, "Homily 9 on 1 Timothy," in *Homilies on the Epistles to the Galatians, Ephesians, Philippians, Colossians, Thessalonians, Timothy, Titus, and Philemon,* ed. and trans. Philip Schaff, *NPNF* 1/13.

childbirth. It also solves the grammatical issue of "she . . . they" if "she" was in quotes and "they" was part of Paul's commentary on the quote.

Does Paul usually place the pronouncement "this is a trustworthy statement" at the beginning of such sayings or at the end? Let's look at his placements of the phrase.

> *At the beginning*: This saying is trustworthy and deserves full acceptance: "Christ Jesus came into the world to save sinners"—and I am the worst of them! (1 Tim 1:15)

> *At the beginning*: This saying is trustworthy:
>
>> If we died with him, we will also live with him.
>> If we endure, we will also reign with him.
>> If we deny him, he will also deny us.
>> If we are unfaithful, he remains faithful, since he cannot deny
>>   himself. (2 Tim 2:11-13)

> *At the end*: But "when the kindness of God our Savior and his love for mankind appeared, he saved us . . . through Jesus Christ our Savior. And so, since we have been justified by his grace, we become heirs with the confident expectation of eternal life." This saying is trustworthy, and I want you to insist on such truths. (Titus 3:4-8)

Apparently, Paul puts this "trustworthy saying" phrase either before or after the saying he quotes, not all one way or the other.

Joining these textual observations with what is known about Ephesus in the first century and Artemis's role as midwife, one can conclude that Paul may well have been quoting a local proverb about childbirth, perhaps a familiar Artemis-related saying about being delivered—before giving the phrase his own Christianized meaning. By engaging our sanctified imaginations, we can possibly better understand why he might have done so.

Meet Theodora, a fictional woman in Ephesus in the second half of the first century CE. As a Romanized Ionian polytheist, she has no division in her world between religion and everyday life. Belief in a variety of gods with different strengths and weaknesses permeates her life. Her home has idols and altars where she offers prayers to many gods.[45] She views each deity as having geographical connections, and Artemis of the Ephesians presides over the area where Theodora lives. In her world, one month of the year is named for Artemis, and festivals commemorate the goddess's birth. Marriage to an older man came early for Theodora, and the threat of early death looms large in her fears.

Decades earlier, Caesar Augustus had introduced laws designed to increase the population of the dwindling upper class. The *jus trium liberorum* (Latin for "the right of three children") rewarded both freeborn citizens who produced at least three offspring and freed slaves (of either sex) who produced at least four.[46] Thus, society provided Theodora with an incentive to bear children: an increased level of female autonomy. Women with *jus trium liberorum* were no longer subject to guardianship by a male relative.

When Theodora was ready to deliver each of her first two children, she went to the temple of Artemis to pray for the goddess of midwifery to grant her a safe delivery. If the goddess was unwilling, Theodora thought, perhaps Artemis would at least use gentle arrows to spare her, should something go wrong. Lacking medicine to cover pain and in the absence of surgery as an option—Cesarean sections wouldn't come along for another 1,400 years—Theodora had seen her only hope as coming from the mercy of the gods, especially Artemis of the Ephesians, goddess of midwifery.

All had gone well in the past, but now Theodora is pregnant again. This time, her world has been radically altered: Theodora, a Gentile, has become a follower of the Jewish Messiah. She has found ways to talk

---

[45]Unlike YHWH, who allows the worship of no other gods, in the polytheistic world of the Ephesians, many gods were included in one person's worship. According to Trebilco, this included emperors: "The emperors were not a threat to the worship of the diverse deities of the empire; rather, the emperors joined the ranks of the divine and played their own particular role in the realm." Paul Trebilco, *The Early Christians in Ephesus from Paul to Ignatius* (Grand Rapids, MI: Eerdmans, 2007), 32.

[46]"*Jus Trium Liberorum*: Definition and Legal Meaning," *Black's Law Dictionary*, 2nd ed., https://thelaw dictionary.org/jus-trium-liberorum/.

about days of the month without uttering the name of a false god. And she has excused herself from city celebrations honoring a deity in whom she no longer believes.[47] She has endured her friends' accusations of betrayal and warnings that she will bring judgment on their entire city at the hands of their outraged, neglected deity.[48] Theodora's children have resented staying home as their friends participate in festivals. But her greatest stress is internal. What if she is wrong? If Artemis is real and Jesus isn't Lord, she is vulnerable to demonic powers raging against her. She wrestles with doubt, struggling to believe in Jesus Christ to deliver her through childbearing. She wonders: Does she have enough confidence in the "God not made with hands" that she will risk enraging Artemis?

Gillman considers a similar context to that described above, except in the case of Thessalonian believers. She writes that in turning from their idols (1 Thess 1:9), these believers might have felt angst as they faced childbirth. Would they relapse or even apostatize, looking for help from a goddess long thought to deliver them through childbirth? She writes:

> Paul was very likely in an ongoing struggle with his newly converted birthing mothers to usurp the function of the goddesses upon whom they relied; [for the Thessalonians] he had styled himself as the nurse with the nurturing power of the gospel he brought them, assisted by Sylvanus and Timothy.[49]

Similarly, an Ephesian woman in such a position might feel she had given up a major benefit when she shifted her allegiance from Artemis. Arnold describes the perceived loss:

---

[47]Guy MacLean Rogers, *The Mysteries of Artemis of Ephesos* (New Haven, CT: Yale University Press, 2012), 7, notes that Richard Oster has observed: "Artemis' close tie with the city of Ephesus, and because legend reported that it was the site of her nativity, we can be sure that [the natal feast] was one of the largest and most magnificent celebrations in Ephesus's liturgical calendar."

[48]Immendörfer observes, "It was a common belief at the time that the gods would punish those who did no fulfil the cultic or ritual demands" (Immendörfer, *Ephesians and Artemis*, 226).

[49]Florence Morgan Gillman, "Paul, His Nurse Metaphor (1 Thessalonians 2:7), and the Thessalonian Women Who Turned against Their Idols," *Catholic Biblical Quarterly* 84, no. 2 (Apr 2022): 279.

For those who gave her their allegiance, Artemis was a benevolent deity. . . . She was an incredibly powerful deity and would sympathetically use her power on behalf of her devotees. . . . She wielded power and authority over heaven, earth, and even the underworld. This was especially evident over the various kinds of spirits that people feared— astral spirits, underworld spirits (especially those who came as functionaries of curses), and terrestrial spirits (spirits of wildlife and nature). She could break the chains of fate, protect people from various kinds of tormenting spirits, and defend people against spirits coming to bring injury, sickness, plague and harm.[50]

In addition to giving up benefits they saw as coming from the goddess herself, new believers in Ephesus risked isolation from everyone except other Christ-followers. One could not even join with other monotheists, because Paul was "convincing them about the kingdom of God. But when some were stubborn and refused to believe, reviling the Way before the congregation, he [Paul] left them and took the disciples with him, addressing them every day in the lecture hall of Tyrannus" (Acts 19:8-9).[51]

As if all these challenges were not enough, Gillman suggests an even more complicated scenario in addition to pressure from children, friends, and the state: the wife whose husband embraced Christ and the enslaved woman whose owner chose to follow Jesus would have been required to convert with the entire household. Such a woman would wonder whether the goddess who aided those in childbirth would still come to her assistance. Gillman envisions such a woman's dilemma:

One might posit that the newly converted birthing mother might secretly, subversively pray interiorly to her former goddesses. Even so, that would be to fail to observe the importance of ritual and materiality in many traditional religious practices. For such a woman we must

---

[50]Arnold, *Ephesians Commentary*, 31-32.
[51]Gillman, "Nurse Metaphor," 285.

suppose that she had been taught that some demonstration, such as visits prior to the birth or post-birth to a site of goddess worship or possession of some physical, material demonstration of attachment to her deities was necessary. That could have taken the form of, for example, purchasing amulets to leave at a site of goddess veneration or to hold during the birth. Thus, one form of syncretism or recidivism I suspect Paul very likely had to counter was the Thessalonian female believers' dependence on goddesses expressed via the possession or offering of amulets.[52]

Consider the possibility of a similar situation in Ephesus to that in Thessalonica. Paul had to combat the loss of Gentiles' perceived benefits from their gods when new believers turned away from idols. If, by telling the Ephesian women that they will be "saved through childbearing" (1 Tim 2:15 NIV), Paul was emphasizing a benefit where one was perceived as lost, he was providing an incentive to trust. The apostle knew his earliest converts were "very likely inclined to try to cover all their bases, bowing to social pressure from both around and within themselves by honoring, surreptitiously, if necessary, any *kourotrophic* [inclined to protect the young] goddesses who might help as they faced the daunting experience of childbirth."[53]

Artemis of the Ephesians was perceived to hold the power to reverse a bad fate, heal sickness, heal safely, or—if one must die—provide a painless, quick death. Belief in such a deity would have provided great comfort in a world in which people were helpless against the slow, agonizing death of mother and/or child when labor failed to progress. Consider the hope offered in Paul's words that such women "will be saved through childbearing—if they continue in faith, love and holiness with propriety" (1 Tim 2:15 NIV).

Our fictional Theodora was just such a woman whose loyalty shifted from following Artemis to following Christ; she would have faced an

---

[52]Gillman, "Nurse Metaphor," 288.
[53]Gillman, "Nurse Metaphor," 294.

enormous adjustment. She would have been going from a female-dominated cult to a more male-dominated one. And she would have been shifting her view of the kind of deliverance for which she would pray. Neglecting the goddess and refusing to make offerings to her in an area that related to this goddess's reputed strength likely would have caused great anxiety for a woman who feared supernatural vengeance.

Refusing to make offerings to the goddess of midwifery as a statement of her newfound faith would likely have caused an Ephesian wife great anxiety. But because Christ is superior to Artemis, it's entirely plausible that Paul was assuring his protégé that believing Ephesian women did not need the goddess of midwifery. Rather, a woman who converted from worshiping Artemis to following Jesus would be saved (delivered) safely—assuming that she lived for Christ.

Bringing it all together, the evidence supports the idea that in saying "she will be saved through [the] childbearing," the author of 1 Timothy was quoting a local proverb, perhaps a familiar Artemis saying. Paul was writing to his protégé, Timothy, who was living in a culture in which Artemis of the Ephesians was esteemed as a midwife who could euthanize or deliver women in labor. The goddess's temple was one of the Seven Wonders of the World, and people came from across the empire to worship her. A conflict existed between her followers and the struggling sect of Judaism known as *the Way*—later *Christianity*—as seen in the book of Acts.

Paul was likely addressing a local problem, and his doing so has often been universalized. Indeed, the author's corrective does have universal implications, but this is *not* one of them: that women are inferior as teachers because of their vulnerability to corruption and should thus never publicly teach men but instead were made to marry, raise children, and limit their teachings to those in the home.

Paul's phrase about women being "saved through childbearing" seems to borrow its structure from the Genesis narrative about the fall and woman's consequence. He alludes to salvation brought through Christ, but he does so by borrowing a local saying. The apostle makes a promise about deliverance in a temporal context for a specific group with a specific challenge to their newfound faith. He does not root the male-female telos only in the Garden of Eden but also in the kingdom of God to come. And he does *not* appear to mean that all believing women everywhere will survive childbirth.

I had set out to test the Kroegers' theory about Artemis as a mothering fertility goddess. The evidence reveals that Artemis was connected not with fertility but virginity; she is nobody's mother. Yet the Kroegers were correct in this: Artemis and her cult, with its Amazon, occult, and magic influences, were the context in which Paul was instructing Timothy.

The focus of my research has been to answer a different question than "can a woman teach men in the church today?" Instead, my objective has been twofold: (1) To discern whether a local situation was likely on Paul's mind when he wrote to Timothy about women, especially about childbearing; and (2) To know whether a woman with a teaching gift is limited to applying it in childbearing.

Seeing Paul's exhortation to Timothy as a local issue with theological ramifications for the universal church about how to handle false teaching reconciles a tension between prohibiting women from teaching the Scriptures in public and the many times God called women to prophesy in every era in which God also has raised up male prophets—including the eras of the Law, kings, post-exilic, pre-Pentecost, Pentecost, and church age. We know too that women will publicly prophesy in the last days in mixed public audiences—not as a sign of the failure of manhood but as a sign of the Holy Spirit (Joel 2:28-29; Acts 2:17-21).

Studying the book of 1 Timothy, especially Paul's instructions about women, in its cultural context sheds light on how Timothy probably received Paul's words and how readers today should take heed. The problem was with specific groups and the turmoil they caused, combined with the falsehoods they passed on. They needed to pray. To stop false teaching. To live in quietness. To learn. And to replace a human-made idol of a midwife with Christ the King, the believer's inheritance: Christ the Lord, God and Savior in the flesh made manifest.

> This is what the LORD says:
> "For the eunuchs who observe my Sabbaths
> and choose what pleases me
> and are faithful to my covenant,
> I will set up within my temple and my walls a monument
> that will be better than sons and daughters.
> I will set up a permanent monument for them that will remain."
> (Is 56:4-5)

ACKNOWLEDGMENTS

THANK YOU TO . . .

Gary, my love for more than four decades, for believing in me and my work and partnering in every way, including provision of meals, errands, encouragement, and weekend getaways so I could write; John Grassmick and the faculty development committee at my alma mater, whose investment in me two decades ago still bears fruit; the late Doris Prince, for her financial sacrifice that became part of the grant that allowed me to update this work; Michelle Nickerson at Loyola University for lending her historical expertise; Anna Moseley Gissing, who first approached me about publishing this content; Jon-not-John Boyd at IVP, who provided great counsel with good cheer; Rebecca Carhart and Abby Stocker for lending their expertise; Debbie Hunn, for handling interlibrary loan requests; Kim Till, for arranging a way for me to get back to Ephesus; Karen and Barney Giesen, for providing a lake house and time away to concentrate; Dorian Coover-Cox, for arranging the New Testament anthropology lecture and always sending good ideas my way; Hall Harris, for directing me to Anatolian studies; Andrew Bartlett, for essential articles; Joe Fantin, for photos and footnote materials that expedited documentation; Sue Edwards, for photos and cheerleading; Heather Goodman, Rachael Gutknecht, Victoria Augas, Kelley Mathews, Peggy McKinnon, the late Bill Cutrer, Misty Hedrick, and Beverly Lucas, for providing invaluable feedback; Steve Smith, Rachel Hannusch, and David Hurst, stellar interns, for serving joyfully and providing great help; Harry Glahn, my father-in-law, for always making sure I could pursue higher ed; Ann Grafe and Anna Piepenburg, my late mother and mother-in-law, for prayers and support; my Adult Bible Fellowship at Centerpoint, especially Rachael for meals, along with Seana Scott, Kelley Mathews, Mary DeMuth, and Rebecca Carrell, for regular prayers and fierce love.

ABBREVIATIONS

FiE   *Forschungen in Ephesos*

IEph.   Wankel, Hermann, et al., eds. *Die Inschriften von Ephesos.* 8 vols. in 11. IK 11–17. Bonn: Habelt, 1979–1984.

IvE   Wankel, Hermann, et al., eds. *Die Inschriften von Ephesos.* 8 vols. in 11. IK 11–17. Bonn: Habelt, 1979–1984 as found in Baugh.

JOAI   *Jahreshefte des Osterreichischen Archäologischen* Institutes in Wien

MM   J. H. Moulton and G. Milligan, *The Vocabulary of the Greek Testament Illustrated from the Papyri and Other Non-Literary Sources*

NPNF   *A Select Library of Nicene and Post-Nicene Fathers of the Christian Church.* Edited by Philip Schaff and Henry Wace. 28 vols. in 2 series. 1886–1889.

SEG   Supplementum Epigraphicum Graecum

SGI   Searchable Greek Inscriptions, The Packard Humanities Institute; "Eph" specifies inscriptions found in "Ionia/Ephesos"

TDNT   *Theological Dictionary of the New Testament*

BIBLIOGRAPHY

Achilles Tatius. *The Adventures of Leucippe and Clitophon*. Translated by S. Gaselee. New York: G. P. Putnam's Sons, 2017.

Ancient Mysteries: Seven Wonders of the Ancient World. New York: A&E Video, 2005.

Anonymous. "The Acts of John." In *The New Testament Apocrypha II*. Edited by Wilhelm Schneemelcher. Translated by R. McL. Wilson. Louisville, KY: Westminster John Knox Press, 2003.

———. "The Acts of Paul." In *The New Testament Apocrypha II*. Edited by Wilhelm Schneemelcher. Translated by R. McL. Wilson. Louisville, KY: Westminster John Knox Press, 2003.

Aquinas, Thomas. *Summa Theologiae*. Translated by Fathers of the English Dominican Province. 2nd ed. 1920. www.newadvent.org/summa/1092.htm.

Aragona, Jared, trans. "The Myth of Telepinu, Hittite God of Fertility." 2021. https://open.maricopa.edu/worldmythologyvolume1godsandcreation/chapter/the-myth-of-telepinu-hittite-god-of-fertility.

Arnold, Clinton E. *Ephesians*. Zondervan Exegetical Commentary on the New Testament. Volume 10. Grand Rapids, MI: Zondervan, 2010.

———. *Ephesians: Power and Magic: The Concept of Power in Ephesians in Light of Its Historical Setting*. Grand Rapids, MI: Baker Academic, 1992.

Arnsperger, Catherine T. *Two Reformation Women and Their Views of Salvation: Katharina Schütz Zell and Marie Dentière*. Mesquite, TX: Aspire Productions, 2020.

Augustine. *The City of God and Christian Doctrine*. Translated by Philip Schaff. *NPNF* 1/2. https://www.ccel.org/ccel/schaff/npnf102.html.

Bacchylides. *Odes.* Translated by Diane Arnson Svarlien. 1991. www.perseus
.tufts.edu/hopper/text?doc=Perseus%3Atext%3A1999.01.0064%3Abook%3
DEp%3Apoem%3D11.

Bammer, A. "A 'Peripteros' of the Geometric Period in the Artemision of
Ephesus." *Anatolian Studies* 40 (1990): 137-209.

Banner, Lois W. "On Writing Women's History." *Journal of Interdisciplinary
History* 2, no. 2 (Autumn 1971): 347-58.

Bartlett, Andrew. *Men and Women in Christ: Fresh Light from the Biblical Texts.*
London: Inter-Varsity Press, 2019.

Bauer, Walter, William F. Arndt, and F. Wilbur Gingrich. "*chēra* [widow]." In
A Greek-English Lexicon of the New Testament and Other Early Christian Literature.
Chicago: University of Chicago Press, 1957.

Baugh, S. M. "The Apostle among the Amazons." *Westminster Theological Journal*
56 (1994): 153-71.

———. "Cult Prostitution in New Testament Ephesus: A Reappraisal." *Journal
of the Evangelical Theological Society* 42, no. 3 (September 1999): 443-60.

———. "A Foreign World: Ephesus in the First Century." In *Women in the Church: An
Analysis and Application of 1 Timothy 2:9-15.* 2nd ed. Edited by Andreas J. Köstenberger and Thomas R. Schreiner. Grand Rapids, MI: Baker Academic, 2005.

Beard, M., and J. Henderson. "With This Body I Thee Worship: Sacred Prostitution in Antiquity." *Gender & History* 9, no. 3 (November 1997): 480-503.

Belleville, Linda L. "Teaching and Usurping Authority." In *Discovering Biblical
Equality,* 2nd ed., edited by Ronald W. Pierce and Rebecca Merrill
Groothuis, 205-23. Downers Grove, IL: InterVarsity Press, 2004.

Bonaventure, *Commentarium in IV Libros Sententiarum Magistri Petri Lombardi.* https://womenpriests.org/theology/bonav1-bonaventure/.

Bourbonnais, Nicole. "A Brief History of Women's History." *Engenderings*
(blog). London School of Economics, March 29, 2016. https://blogs.lse
.ac.uk/gender/2016/03/29/a-brief-history-of-womens-history/.

Brenk, Frederick E. "Artemis of Ephesos: An *Avant Garde* Goddess." *Kernos* 11
(1998): 157-71.

Brown, Peter. *The Body and Society: Men, Women, and Sexual Renunciation in
Early Christianity.* New York: Columbia University Press, 1988.

Budin, Stephanie. *The Myth of Sacred Prostitution in Antiquity.* New York: Cambridge University Press, 2008.

Burnett, D. Clint. *Studying the New Testament Through Inscriptions: An Introduction.* Peabody, MA: Hendrickson Academic, 2020.

Bunsen, Matthew. *Encyclopedia of the Roman Empire.* New York: Facts on File, 1994.

Callimachus. *Works.* Translated by A. W. Mair. London: William Heinemann, 1921.

Chrysostom, John. "Homily 9 on 1 Timothy." In *Homilies on the Epistles to the Galatians, Ephesians, Philippians, Colossians, Thessalonians, Timothy, Titus, and Philemon.* Edited and translated by Philip Schaff. *NPNF* 1/13.

Coffman, James Burton. *Commentary on 1 Corinthians 11.* Coffman's Commentaries on the Bible. Abilene, TX: Abilene Christian University Press, 1983–1999.

Cohick, Lynn H. *Women in the World of the Earliest Christians: Illuminating Ancient Ways of Life.* Grand Rapids, MI: Baker Academic, 2009.

Cohick, Lynn, and Amy Brown Hughes. *Christian Women in the Patristic World: Their Influence, Authority, and Legacy in the Second Through Fifth Centuries.* Grand Rapids, MI: Baker Academic, 2017.

Cook, Arthur B. "The Bee in Greek Mythology." *The Journal of Hellenic Studies* 15 (1895): 1-24.

———. *Zeus: A Study in Ancient Religion.* Volume 3. Cambridge: Cambridge University Press, 1940.

Cornelius Tacitus. *Annales ab excessu divi Augusti.* Translated by Charles Dennis Fisher. Oxford: Clarendon Press, 1906.

Council for Biblical Manhood and Womanhood. "The Danvers Statement." https://cbmw.org/about/danvers-statement/.

Desjardins, Michel. "The Apocryphon of Jannes and Jambres the Magicians: P. Chester Beatty XVI." *The Journal of the American Oriental Society* 116, no. 3 (July–Sept 1996): 562-63.

De Haas, Ingrid. "Roman Magic: Control in an Uncertain World." *The Ultimate History Project.* May 7, 2020. https://ultimatehistoryproject.com/roman-magic-amulets-bullae-lunulae.html.

de Pizan, Christine. *The Book of the City of Ladies (Le Livre de la Cité des Dames)*. Translated by Earl Jeffrey Richards. New York: Persea Books, 1982.

Dio Chrysostom. *Orations*. Translated by Henry Lamar Crosby. Loeb Classical Library. Cambridge, MA: Harvard University Press, 1940.

Diodorus of Sardis, *The Greek Anthology III*. In *Select Epigrams from the Greek Anthology*. Edited by J. W. Mackail. London: Longmans, Green, and Co., 1890.

Dzubinski, Leanne M., and Anneke H. Stasson. *Women in the Mission of the Church: Their Opportunities and Obstacles Throughout Christian History*. Grand Rapids, MI: Baker Academic, 2021.

Eckhart, TammyJo. "An Author-Centered Approach to Understanding Amazons in the Ancient World." PhD diss., Indiana University, 2007.

Edwards, Sue, and Kelley Mathews. *40 Questions About Women in Public Ministry*. Grand Rapids, MI: Kregel Academic, 2022.

Eisen, Ute E. *Women Officeholders in Early Christianity: Epigraphical and Literary Studies*. Translated by Linda Maloney. Collegeville, MN: Liturgical Press, 2000.

Elm, Susanna. *Virgins of God: The Making of Asceticism in Late Antiquity*. Oxford: Clarendon Press, 1994.

Erasmus. *Collected Works of Erasmus: Paraphrases on the Epistles to Timothy, Titus and Philemon, the Epistles of Peter and Jude, the Epistle of James, the Epistles of John, and the Epistle to the Hebrews*. Translated by John J. Bateman. Edited by R. D. Sider. Toronto: University of Toronto Press, 1994.

Euripides. *Hippolytus*. Translated by Ian Johnston. 2020. http://johnstoniatexts .x10host.com/euripides/hippolytushtml.html.

Fantham, Elaine, Helene Peet Foley, Natalie Boymel Kampen, and Sarah B. Pomeroy. *Women in the Classical World: Image and Text*. New York: Oxford University Press, 1995.

Fieger, Michael. *Im Schatten der Artemis: Glaube und Ungehorsam in Ephesus*. Berlin: Peter Lang Group Internationaler Verlag der Wissenschaften, 1998.

Fell, Margaret. *Women's Speaking Justified, Proved, and Allowed of By the Scriptures, All Such as Speak by the Spirit and Power of the Lord Jesus*. London: Society of Friends, 1666.

Ferguson, Everett. *Backgrounds of Early Christianity*. 2nd ed. Grand Rapids, MI: Eerdmans, 1993.

Ferguson, James. *The Temple of Diana at Ephesus: With Especial Reference to Mr. Woods' Discoveries of Its Remains.* London: Trübner and Company, 1883.

Fleischer, R. *Artemis von Ephesus und Verwandte Kultstatuen aus Anatolien und Syrien.* EPRO 35. Leiden: Brill, 1973.

Foley, Helene. *Reflections of Women in Antiquity.* New York: Routledge, 1992.

Foreman, Amanda. "The Amazon Women: Is There Any Truth Behind the Myth?" *Smithsonian Magazine*, April 2014. www.smithsonianmag.com /history/amazon-women-there-any-truth-behind-myth-180950188/.

Friesen, Steven J. *Imperial Cults and the Apocalypse of John: Reading Revelation in the Ruins.* Oxford: Oxford Academic, 2001.

———. *Twice* Neokoros: *Ephesus, Asia and the Cult of the Flavian Imperial Family.* Leiden: Brill, 1993.

Frontinus. *Stratagems, Aqueducts.* Translated by Charles E. Bennett. Loeb Classical Library. Cambridge, MA: Harvard University Press, 1925.

Fulda, Joseph S. "The Internet as an Engine of Scholarship." *Computers and Society* 30, no. 1 (March 2000): 17-27.

Gardner, Jane F. "Proofs of Status in the Roman World." *Bulletin of the Institute of Classical Studies*, no. 33 (1986): 1-14.

———. *Women in Roman Law and Society.* Bloomington, IN: Indiana University Press, 1986.

Gillman, Florence Morgan. "Paul, His Nurse Metaphor (1 Thessalonians 2:7), and the Thessalonian Women Who Turned against Their Idols." *Catholic Biblical Quarterly* 84, no. 2 (Apr 2022): 279-94.

Glahn, Sandra L. "The First-Century Ephesian Artemis: Ramifications of Her Identity." *Bibliotheca Sacra* 172, no. 688 (October–December 2015): 450-69.

———. "The Identity of Artemis in First-Century Ephesus." *Bibliotheca Sacra* 172 (July–Sept 2015): 316-34.

———. "Not with Braided Hair . . . or Pearls." *Engage* (blog). Bible.org, December 10, 2010. https://blogs.bible.org/not-with-braided-hair-or-pearls/, accessed February 27, 2023.

———. "*1 Timothy*: A Review," *Bibliotheca Sacra* 172, no. 686 (Apr–Jun 2015) 248-50.

————. "The 'Widow' in the Early Church: Marital Demarcation, Office Title, or Both?" Paper presented at the annual meeting of the Evangelical Theological Society, Fort Worth, Texas, November 18, 2021, www.wordmp3.com/details.aspx?id=40733.

Gleiser, Marcelo. "Does Technology Make You Freer?" *Cosmos & Culture* (blog). NPR.org, October 21, 2015. www.npr.org/sections/13.7/2015/10/21/450473648/does-technology-make-you-freer.

Graf, Fritz. "An Oracle Against Pestilence from a Western Anatolian Town." *Zeitschrift für Papyrologie und Epigraphik* 92 (1992): 267-79.

Grudem, Wayne. *Evangelical Feminism and Biblical Truth*. Sisters, OR: Multnomah, 2004.

Gryson, Roger. *The Ministry of Women in the Early Church*. Collegeville, MN: Liturgical Press, 1976.

Hazel, John. *Who's Who in the Greek World*. New York: Routledge, 2000.

Herculaneum Uncovered: Secrets of the Dead. 60 minutes. Arlington, VA: PBS Home Video, 2004.

Herodotus. *The History of Herodotus*. Translated by G. C. Macaulay. Vol. 1. New York: MacMillan, 1890. www.gutenberg.org/files/2707/2707-h/2707-h.htm#link2H_4_0004.

————. *The Histories*. Translated by Aubrey de Sélincourt. New York: Penguin Books, 2003.

Hesiod. *Homeric Hymns, Epic Cycle, Homerica*. Translated by Hugh G. Evelyn-White. Loeb Classical Library. Cambridge, MA: Harvard University Press, 1914.

Hesiod. *Theogony*, 901 in *The Homeric Hymns and Homerica*. Translated by Hugh G. Evelyn-White. Cambridge, MA: Harvard University Press; London, William Heinemann Ltd. 1914. www.perseus.tufts.edu/hopper/text?doc=Perseus%3Atext%3A1999.01.0130%3Acard%3D901, Accessed February 27, 2023.

Hill, Andrew E. "Ancient Art and Artemis: Explaining the Polymastic Nature of the Figurine." *Journal of Ancient Near Eastern Studies* 21 (1992): 91-94.

Hoag, Gary G. *Wealth in Ancient Ephesus and the First Letter of Timothy: Fresh Insights from Ephesiaca by Xenophon of Ephesus*. Bulletin for Biblical Research, Supplement II. Winona Lake, IN: Eisenbrauns, 2015.

Hölbl, Günther. *Zeugnisse ägyptischer Religionsvorstellungen für Ephesus.* Études préliminaires aux religions orientales dans l'Empire romain, vol. 73. Leiden: Brill, 1978.

Homer. *Homeri Opera in Five Volumes.* Oxford: Oxford University Press, 1920.

———. *The Homeric Hymns and Homerica.* Translated by Hugh G. Evelyn-White. Cambridge, MA: Harvard University Press, 1914.

———. *The Iliad.* Translated by E. V. Rieu. New York: Penguin, 2003.

———. *The Iliad with an English Translation by A.T. Murray, Ph.D., in Two Volumes.* Cambridge, MA: Harvard University Press, 1924.

———. *The Odyssey with an English Translation.* Translated by A. T. Murray. Cambridge, MA: Harvard University Press, 1919.

Horsley, G. H. R. "The Inscriptions of Ephesos and the New Testament." *Novum Testamentum* 34, no. 2 (April 1992): 105-68.

Hübner, Jamin. *A Case for Female Deacons.* Eugene, OR: Wipf and Stock, 2015.

———. "Patriarchy Rears Its Head (Again)." *Scot's Newsletter*, May 12, 2021. https://scotmcknight.substack.com/p/patriarchy-rears-its-head-again.

———. "Revisiting αὐθεντέω in 1 Timothy 2:12: What Do the Extant Data Really Show?" *Journal for the Study of Paul and His Letters* 5, no. 1 (Summer 2015): 41-70.

Immendörfer, Michael. *Ephesians and Artemis: The Cult of the Great Goddess of Ephesus as the Epistle's Context.* Wissenschaftliche Untersuchungen zum Neuen Testament II 436. Tübingen, Germany: Mohr Siebeck, 2017.

Jacobs, Maretha M. "On Fairness and Accuracy in the Academy: A Brief Response to Wim Vergeer's Use of Terminologies, and Some Simplifications, in the Article 'The Redeemer in an "Irredeemable Text" (1 Tim. 2:9-15).'" *Neotestamentica* 51, no. 2 (2017): 359-65.

Jordan, D. R. "A Love Charm with Verses." *Zeitschrift für Papyrologie und Epigraphik* 72 (1988): 245-59.

Jenny-Kappers, Theodora. *Muttergöttin und Gottesmutter in Ephesos: von Artemis zu Maria* [*Mother Goddess and Mother of God in Ephesos: from Artemis to Mary*]. Einsiedeln, Switzerland: Daimon, 1986.

Jerome. "Prologue to *Commentary on the Epistle to the Ephesians.*" (*Commentarius in Epistolam ad Ephesios,*) PL26, https://epistolae.ctl.columbia.edu/letter/283.html.

Johnson, Lewis S. "Role Distinctions in the Church: Galatians 3:28." In *Recovering Biblical Manhood and Womanhood: A Response to Evangelical Feminism*, edited by John Piper and Wayne Grudem, 154-64. Wheaton, IL: Crossway, 2021.

Johnson, Marguerite. "The Grim Reality of the Brothels of Pompeii." *The Conversation*, December 12, 2017, https://theconversation.com/the-grim -reality-of-the-brothels-of-pompeii-88853.

Karaman, Elif Hilal. *Ephesian Women in Greco-Roman and Early Christian Perspective*. Tübingen: Mohr Siebeck, 2018.

Keller, Kathy. *Jesus, Justice, and Gender Roles: A Case for Gender Roles in Ministry*. Fresh Perspectives on Women in Ministry. Grand Rapids, MI: Zondervan, 2012.

Kittel, Gerhard, and Gerhard Friedrich, eds. *Theological Dictionary of the New Testament*. Translated by Geoffrey W. Bromiley. 10 vols. Grand Rapids, MI: Eerdmans, 1964–1976.

Knox, John. *The First Blast of the Trumpet against the Monstrous Regiment of Women*. 1558. Reprint, London: 1878. www.gutenberg.org/files/9660 /9660-h/9660-h.htm.

Koester, Helmut. *Ephesos: Metropolis of Asia: An Interdisciplinary Approach*. Harrisburg, PA: Trinity Press, 1995.

Köstenberger, Andreas J., and Thomas R. Schreiner, eds. *Women in the Church: An Analysis and Application of 1 Timothy 2:9-15*. 2nd ed. Grand Rapids, MI: Baker Academic, 2005.

Kraemer, Ross. "The Other as Woman: An Aspect of Polemic Among Pagans, Jews and Christians in the Greco-Roman World." In *The Other in Jewish Thought and History: Constructions of Jewish Culture and Identity*, edited by Laurence J. Silberstein and Robert L. Cohn, 50-79. New York: NYU Press, 1994.

Kroeger, Richard Clark, and Katherine Clark Kroeger. *I Suffer Not a Woman: Rethinking 1 Timothy 2:11-15 in Light of Ancient Evidence*. Grand Rapids, MI: Baker, 1992.

Laale, Hans Willer. *Ephesus (Ephesos): An Abbreviated History from Androclus to Constantine XI*. Nashville: Westbow Press, 2021.

Lavoipierre, Frederique. "Garden Allies: Honey Bees." Pacific Horticulture. www.pacifichorticulture.org/articles/honey-bees.

Léger, Ruth Marie. "Artemis and Her Cult." PhD diss., University of Birmingham, April 2015.

Lehmann-Hartleben, Karl L. H. "The Amazon Group." *Parnassus* 8, no. 4 (April 1936): 9-11.

Lerner, Gerda. "Priorities and Challenges in Women's History Research." *Perspectives on History*, American Historical Association, April 1, 1988, www.historians.org/research-and-publications/perspectives-on-history/april-1988/priorities-and-challenges-in-womens-history-research.

Levin-Richardson, Sarah. *The Brothel of Pompeii: Sex, Class, and Gender at the Margins of Roman Society.* Cambridge: Cambridge University Press, 2019.

LiDonnici, Lynn R. "The Images of Artemis Ephesia and Greco-Roman Worship: A Reconsideration." *Harvard Theological Review* 85, no. 4 (Oct 1992): 389-415.

Longfellow, Brenda. *Roman Imperialism and Civic Patronage: Form, Meaning, and Ideology in Monumental Fountain Complexes.* Cambridge: Cambridge University Press, 2014.

Luther, Martin. *Lectures on 1 Timothy.* In *Luther's Works,* vol. 28. Edited by Hilton C. Oswald. St Louis: Concordia, 1973.

Madigan, Kevin, and Carolyn Osiek. *Ordained Women in the Early Church: A Documentary History.* Baltimore, MD: Johns Hopkins University Press, 2011.

Martimort, A. Georges. *Deaconesses: An Historical Study.* Translated by K. D. Whitehead. San Francisco: Ignatius Press, 1986.

McBride, Bunny. "Ephesus." *The Christian Science Monitor.* May 7, 1986. www.csmonitor.com/1986/0507/zephe-f.html.

McKnight, Scot. *The Blue Parakeet: Rethinking How You Read the Bible.* 2nd ed. Grand Rapids, MI: Zondervan, 2018.

Metzger, Bruce M. *A Textual Commentary on the Greek New Testament.* 2nd ed. Stuttgard, Germany: German Bible Society, 1994.

Metzger, E. "The Case of Petronia Iusta." *Revue Internationale des Droit de l'Antiquité (3rd series)* 47 (2000): 151-65.

Minucius Felix. *The Octavius.* Translated by Robert Ernest Wallis. https://ccel.org/ccel/felix/octavius/anf04.iv.iii.xxi.html.

Morford, Mark, and Robert Lenardon. *Classical Mythology.* New York: Oxford University Press, 2003.

Morris, Sarah P. "The Prehistoric Background of Artemis Ephesia: A Solution to the Enigma of Her 'Breasts'?" *Der Kosmos der Artemis von Ephesos. Sonderschriften des Österreichischen Archäologischen Instituts* 37 (2001): 135-51.

"Mortality in the United States: Past, Present, and Future." *Penn Wharton Budget Model.* June 27, 2016. https://budgetmodel.wharton.upenn.edu /issues/2016/1/25/mortality-in-the-united-states-past-present-and-future.

Mowczko, Marg. "The Regalia of Artemis Ephesia." *Marg Mowczko.* July 23, 2016. https://margmowczko.com/regalia-artemis-ephesia/.

Murphy-O'Connor, Jerome. *St. Paul's Ephesus: Texts and Archaeology.* Collegeville, MN: Liturgical Press, 2008.

Murray, A. S. "Remains of Archaic Temple of Artemis at Ephesus." *The Journal of Hellenic Studies* 10 (1889): 1-10.

Muss, Ulrike. "The Artemision in Early Christian Times." *Early Christianity* 7 (2016): 293-312.

Myers, Nancy. "Cicero's (S)Trumpet: Roman Women and the Second Philippic." *Rhetoric Review* 22, no. 4 (2003): 337-52.

Nortjé-Meyer, L. "Die hiërargiese funksionering van God, mans en vroue in die brief aan die Efersiërs." *Verbum et Ecclesia* 21, no. 1 (2003): 180-93.

Nortjé-Meyer, Lilly (S. J.), and Alta Vrey. "Artemis as Matrix for a New Interpretation of the Household Codes in Ephesians 5:22-6:9." *Neotestamentica* 50, no. 1 (2016): 53-70.

O'Sullivan, James N. "Preliminary." In *Xenophon of Ephesus.* New York: Walter de Gruyter, 1994.

Oakley, K. P. "The *Diopet* of Ephesus." *Folklore* 82, no. 3 (Autumn 1971): 207-11.

Olson, Kelly. *Dress and the Roman Woman: Self-Presentation and Society.* New York: Routledge, 2008.

Oster, Richard. "The Ephesian Artemis 'Whom All Asia and the World Worship' (Acts 19:27): Representative Epigraphical Testimony to Ἄρτεμις Ἐφεσία outside Ephesos," in *Transmission and Reception: New Testament Text-Critical and Exegetical Studies,* edited by J. W. Childers and D. C. Parker, 212-31. Piscataway, NJ: Gorgias Press, 2006.

———. "Ephesus as a Religious Center under the Principate, I. Paganism before Constantine," in *Aufstieg und Niedergang der Römischen Welt,* edited by

Wolfgang Haase and Hildegard Temporini, 1661-1728. New York: Walter de Gruyter, 1990.

———. "Other Books." *The Biblical Archaeologist* 56, no. 4 (December 1993): 225-27.

Ovid. *Metamorphoses*. Translated by A. S. Kline. 2000. www.poetryintranslation .com/PITBR/Latin/Metamorph3.php#anchor_Toc64106183.

———. *Metamorphoses*. Translated by Hugo Magnus. Gotha, Germany: F. A. Perthes. 1892.

Pausanias. *Description of Greece*. Translated by W. H. S. Jones. Loeb Classical Library. Cambridge, MA: Harvard University Press, 1978.

Payne, Philip. *Man and Woman, One in Christ: An Exegetical and Theological Study of Paul's Letters*. Grand Rapids, MI: Zondervan, 2009.

———. "1 Tim 2.12 and the Use of οὐδέ to Combine Two Elements to Express a Single Idea." *New Testament Studies* 54, no. 2 (2008): 235-53.

Peppiatt, Lucy. *Rediscovering Scripture's Vision for Women: Fresh Perspectives on Disputed Texts*. Downers Grove, IL: InterVarsity Press, 2017.

———. *Women and Worship at Corinth: Paul's Rhetorical Arguments in 1 Corinthians*. Eugene, OR: Cascade Books, 2015.

Pierce, Ronald W., Cynthia Long Westfall, and Christa McKirland, eds. *Discovering Biblical Equality*. 3rd ed. Downers Grove, IL: InterVarsity Press, 2021.

Pietersen, Lloyd K. "Women as Gossips and Busybodies? Another look at 1 Timothy 5:13." *Lexington Theological Quarterly* 42, no 1 (Spring 2007): 19-35.

Pindar, *Pythian Ode*, 4.4 in Odes. Translated by Diane Arnson Svarlien. 1990. www.perseus.tufts.edu/hopper/text?doc=Perseus%3Atext%3A1999.01.0162 %3Abook%3DP.%3Apoem%3D4, accessed February 27, 2023.

Piper, John, and Wayne Grudem, eds. *Recovering Biblical Manhood and Womanhood: A Response to Evangelical Feminism*. Wheaton, IL: Crossway, 2006.

Plato. *Plato in Twelve Volumes*. Translated by Harold N. Fowler. Loeb Classical Library. Cambridge, MA: Harvard University Press, 1921.

Pliny the Elder. *The Natural History*. Translated by John Bostock and H. T. Riley. London: Taylor and Francis, 1855.

Plutarch. "The Life of Alexander." In *The Parallel Lives*. Translated by Frank Cole Babbitt. Loeb Classical Library. Cambridge, MA: Harvard University Press, 1919.

Pomeroy, Sarah B. *Families in Classical and Hellenistic Greece: Representations and Realities.* Oxford: Clarendon, 1996.

———. *Goddesses, Whores, Wives, and Slaves: Women in Classical Antiquity.* New York: Schocken Books, 1975.

Pyne, Robert A. "I Suffer Not a Woman: Rethinking 1 Timothy 2:11-15 in Light of Ancient Evidence." *Bibliotheca Sacra* 150, no. 598 (Apr–Jun 1993): 247-48.

Ransome, Hilda M. The *Sacred Bee in Ancient Times and Folklore.* London: George Allen & Unwin, 1937.

Robertson, Martin. *The Eye of Greece: Studies in the Art of Athens.* Cambridge: Cambridge University Press, 1982.

Rogers, Guy MacLean. "The Constructions of Women at Ephesos." *Zeitschrift für Papyrologie und Epigraphik* 90 (1992): 215-23.

———. *The Mysteries of Artemis of Ephesos.* New Haven, CT: Yale University Press, 2012.

Saucy, Robert L., and Judith K. TenElshof, eds. *Women and Men in Ministry: A Complementary Perspective.* Chicago: Moody Publishers, 2001.

Schiff, Stacy. *Cleopatra: A Life.* New York: Little, Brown, 2010.

Schmitz, Matthew. "Texas Bible Converts 'You' to 'Y'all.'" *First Things* (blog), June 3, 2013. www.firstthings.com/blogs/firstthoughts/2013/06/texas-bible -converts-you-to-yall.

Schroeder, Joy A. and Marion Ann Taylor. *Voices Long Silenced: Women Biblical Interpreters Through the Centuries.* Louisville, KY: Westminster John Knox, 2022.

Schwindt, Rainer. *Das Weltbild des Epheserbriefes: Eine religionsgeschichtlich-exegetische Studie.* Wissenschaftliche Untersuchungen zum Neuen Testament 148. Tübingen: Mohr Siebeck, 2002.

Searchable Greek Inscriptions. The Packard Humanities Institute. http:// epigraphy.packhum.org.

Seltman, Charles. "The Wardrobe of Artemis." *The Numismatic Chronicle and the Journal of the Royal Numismatic Society (Sixth Series)* 12, no. 42 (1952): 33-44.

Seneca. *Letters.* Translated by Richard M. Gummere. Loeb Classical Library. Cambridge: Harvard University Press, 1925.

———. *Tragedies.* Translated by Frank Justus Miller. Loeb Classical Library. Cambridge: Harvard University Press, 1917.

Siekierka, Przemysław, Krystyna Stebnicka, and Aleksander Wolicki. *Women and the Polis: Public Honorific Inscriptions for Women in the Greek Cities from the Late Classical to the Roman Period.* 2 volumes. Berlin: De Gruyter, 2021.

Sokolowski, F. "A New Testimony on the Cult of Artemis of Ephesus." *Harvard Theological Review* 58, no. 4 (1965): 427-31.

Spencer, Aída Besançon. *1 Timothy.* New Covenant Commentary Series. Eugene, OR: Cascade Books, 2013.

Statius. *Thebaid.* Translated by A. D. Melville. Oxford: Oxford University Press, 1992.

Strabo. *Geography.* Translated by Horace L. Jones. Loeb Classical Library. Cambridge, MA: Harvard University Press, 1949.

Strelan, Rick. *Paul, Artemis, and the Jews in Ephesus.* New York: Walter de Gruyter, 1996.

Tacitus. *Annals.* Translated by John Jackson. Loeb Classical Library. Cambridge, MA: Harvard University Press, 1937.

Tellbe, Mikael. *Christ-Believers in Ephesus. A Textual Analysis of Early Christian Identity Formation in a Local Perspective.* Wissenschaftliche Untersuchungen Zum Neuen Testament I/242. Tübingen: Mohr Siebeck, 2009.

Thiessen, Werner. *Christen in Ephesus: Die historische und theologische Situation in vorpaulinischer und paulinischer Zeit und zur Zeit der Apostelgeschichte und der Pastoralbriefe.* TANZ 12. Tübingen/Basel: Francke, 1995.

Thurston, Bonnie Bowman. *The Widows: A Women's Ministry in the Early Church.* Minneapolis: Fortress, 1989.

Trebilco, Paul. *The Early Christians in Ephesus from Paul to Ignatius.* Grand Rapids, MI: Eerdmans, 2007.

———. *Jewish Communities in Asia Minor.* Cambridge: Cambridge University Press, 1991.

Trombley, Charles. *Who Said Women Can't Teach?* Gainesville, FL: Bridge-Logos, 1985.

Varone, Antonio. *Eroticism in Pompeii.* Los Angeles: J. Paul Getty Museum, 2001.

Vergeer, W. C. "The Redeemer in an 'Irredeemable Text' (1 Timothy 2:9-15)." *Neotestamentica* 50, no. 1 (2016): 71-87.

Vitruvius. *On Architecture.* Translated by Frank Granger. Loeb Classical Library. Cambridge, MA: Harvard University Press, 1931, 1934.

Wallace, Daniel B. Interview with Sandra Glahn. Dallas, Texas, January 12, 2011.

Warhurst, Margaret. "The Danson Bequest and Merseyside County Museums," *Archaeological Reports* 24 (1977–1978): 85-88.

Weaver, Paul. "Archaeological Discoveries of Ancient Corinth and the Exegesis of First Corinthians: From Archaeology to Exegesis." *The Journal of Ministry & Theology* 23 no. 2 (Fall 2019): 204-205.

Weiss, Harry B. "Swammerdam, Jan Jacobz." *The Scientific Monthly* 25, no. 3 (Sept 1927): 220-27.

Weissenrieder, Annette. "What Does σωθήσεθαι [sic] δὲ διὰ τῆς τεκνογονίας 'to Be Saved by Childbearing' Mean (1 Timothy 2:15)? Insights from Ancient Medical and Philosophical Texts." *Early Christianity* 5 (2014): 313-36.

Westfall, Cynthia Long. *Paul and Gender: Reclaiming the Apostle's Vision for Men and Women in Christ*. Grand Rapids, MI: Baker Academic, 2016.

Williams, Kelly. "Biblical Conservatism and Women Pastors: A Southern Baptist Pastor's Understanding," *The Christian Post*, August 30, 2022.

Winston, George, and Dora Winston. *Recovering Biblical Ministry by Women*. Longwood, FL: Xulon Press, 2003.

Winter, Bruce. *Roman Wives, Roman Widows*. Grand Rapids, MI: Eerdmans, 2003.

Witetschek, Stephan. *Ephesische Enthullungen 1: Fruhe Christen in einer antiken Grosstadt*. Zugleich ein Beitrag zur Frage nach den Kontexten der Johannesapokalypse. Leuven, Belgium: Peeters Publishers, 2008.

Witt, William G. *Icons of Christ: A Biblical and Systematic Theology for Women's Ordination*. Waco, TX: Baylor University Press, 2020.

Wood, J. T. *Discoveries at Ephesus: Including the Site and Remains of the Great Temple of Diana*. New York: Longmans, Green, 1877.

Worrall, Simon. "Amazon Warriors Did Indeed Fight and Die Like Men," *National Geographic*, October 28, 2014. www.nationalgeographic.com/history/ article/141029-amazons-scythians-hunger-games-herodotus-ice-princess -tattoo-cannabis.

Xenophon. *Ephesian History: Or the Love-Adventure of Abrocomas and Anthia*. Translated by Mr. Rooke. 2nd ed. London: J. Millan, 1727.

Zinsser, Judith. *History and Feminism: A Glass Half Full*. New York: Twayne, 1993.

MONOGRAPHS ON EPHESUS AND PAUL'S LETTERS TO TIMOTHY

Significant monographs on Ephesus in chronological order. The starred ones address 1 or 2 Timothy or both.

*Arnold, Clinton E.	1989
*Thiessen, Werner	1995 [in German]
*Strelan, Rick	1996
Fieger, Michael	1998 [in German]
*Hölbl, Günther	1998 [in German]
Schwindt, Rainer	2002 [in German]
*Trebilco, Paul	2007
*Murphy-O'Connor, Jerome	2008
Witetschek, Stephan	2008 [in German]
*Tellbe, Mikael	2009
*Arnold, Clinton E.	2010
*Hoag, Gary G.	2015
*Immendörfer, Michael	2017

GENERAL INDEX

and gold quiver, 88
and gold reins, 46, 55
and gold throne, 46, 55
and hair, 52
and head adornment, 52, 48, 50, 76, 88, 89,
    102-3, 132
and hunting, 40, 45-46, 47, 48, 50, 52, 54,
    55, 56, 59, 64, 65, 73, 74, 88, 101, 102, 105,
    113, 118
as light bringer, 54, 88, 92, 126
as lion, 47, 112
as lord, 49, 55, 56, 57, 86, 92, 94, 117, 118
meaning of name, 63
and men, 56, 59-60, 84
and midwifery, 49, 54, 56, 60, 61, 63, 72, 76,
    77, 79, 80, 88, 89, 99, 113, 115, 116, 143,
    150, 151, 155
and mountains, 46, 50, 54, 57
names derived from, 84-85
and Orion, 59, 79
and painless arrows (euthanasia), 50, 51, 54,
    60, 79, 85, 115, 116, 143, 154, 155
prayers offered to, 57, 74, 75, 84, 116, 153
priestess of, 85, 86-89, 91-97, 115
and protection, 52, 56, 60, 61, 71-72, 77, 83,
    90, 99, 102, 109, 115, 116, 153, 154
as Queen of the Cosmos, 86
as savior, 86, 100, 116, 118, 127
and silver bow, 48, 55
sister/twin of Apollo, 45, 47, 49, 50, 59, 60,
    62, 63, 66, 67, 68, 114, 115
statues of, 52, 70, 86, 92, 100, 101-13
temple of. *See* Artemision
titles of, 34, 55, 57, 68, 69, 86, 117-18, 142
as Upis Queen, 57
and virginity, 49, 50, 51, 53, 55, 57, 58, 59,
    60, 64, 66, 72, 74, 75, 76, 79, 84, 88, 89, 96,
    97, 101, 112, 114, 115, 118, 128, 156
and volatility, 48, 56, 59, 60, 65, 66, 115
as watcher of streets and harbors, 54, 57
and woman killing, 46, 47, 48, 51, 55, 56, 59,
    60, 61, 76, 115
and wrath, 46, 56
Artemision, 35, 37, 38, 43, 51, 66, 68, 71, 72, 75,
    79, 84, 87, 90, 91, 92, 93, 99-102, 106, 108, 109,
    126, 129, 132, 140, 151, 155
artifacts, 44, 72, 101, 103, 112
Asia, province of, 36, 62, 90, 175
astrology, 126
Athena, 49, 69, 77, 83
Augustine of Hippo, 19, 23, 164
Augustus, 35, 135, 151, 153

Aurora, 65
authority, 7, 8, 9, 14, 15, 23, 30, 33, 39, 104, 128,
    129, 137-40, 142, 153
Balbilus, 126
Bammer, Anton, 108, 109
baptism, 22, 24
Baugh, S. M., 53, 61, 66, 78, 80, 86, 87, 95, 96,
    106, 113, 114
beads, 108, 109, 131
bees, 111-13, 170
Bellerophon, 46
Belleville, Linda, 39, 139
biblical women
    Anna, 9
    Corinthian prophets, 9
    Deborah, 9
    Elizabeth, 9
    Huldah, 9
    Julia, 12
    Junia, 9, 11, 12
    Lydia, 6, 68, 71
    Martha of Bethany, 6, 10
    Mary, mother of Jesus, 9, 36, 41, 62, 101
    Miriam, 9, 17
    Nympha, 6
    Persis, 12
    Phillip's daughters, 9, 12
    Prisca/Priscilla, 6, 12, 14, 35, 98
    Tryphena, 12
    Tryphosa, 12, 94, 95
    widows of 1 Timothy 5, 12, 23
bishop, 19, 22, 23, 133
Black Madonna, 62
Black Sea, 41, 42
blood, 25, 31
boar, 46, 50, 58
Bonaventure, 19
Book of the City of Ladies, 22
braids, 8, 127, 128, 130, 131, 133, 135
breadwinner, 3, 6
breasts, 6, 40, 41, 51, 56, 65, 102, 104-8, 110, 114
Briseis, 47
British Museum, 99
Britomartis, 118
Brown, Peter, 61, 164
Budin, Stephanie, 32, 114
bull scrota, 107, 111
burial mounds, 42
    See also kurgans
busybodies, 123, 124, 125
Callimachus, 49, 53, 55-59
celibacy, 12, 52, 76, 96, 115, 124, 128

SCRIPTURE INDEX

ANCIENT WRITINGS INDEX

Printed in the USA
CPSIA information can be obtained
at www.ICGtesting.com
CBHW071219150224
4367CB00003B/112